PRAISE FOR
FIRST-CHOICE LIFE

"*First-Choice Life* is a therapeutic bible of embodied spiritual wisdom. It's a divine declaration of truth for those seeking answers to the persistent inner restlessness and sense that there must be 'something more' that can only come from a second-choice life. Let Thea Rotteveel inspire you to answer your soul's call to reclaim an existence that's nothing less than your first choice."

–Ashley Jordan, JD, journalist, speaker, women's advocate, and author of *Unhappy Achiever: Rejecting the Good Girl Image and Reclaiming the Joy of Inner Fulfillment*

"*First-Choice Life* is a powerful call to action for readers to embrace their individuality, live intentionally, and pursue a life that is true to their essence, ultimately crafting a life that is not just a default option but their first-choice life."

–Tanya Hale, midlife relationship coach, podcaster, *Intentional Living with Tanya Hale*

"If someone writes a book about such an existential topic for all who live first-, second-, or maybe even third-choice lives, there is only one way for the writer to do so: to have lived the journey herself. Thea did! This creates depth and makes the book convincing and useful."

–Peter P. Robertson, MD, corporate consultant, psychiatrist

FIRST-CHOICE LIFE

Advocate for
Your True Self and
Live Your Dreams

THEA ROTTEVEEL

GREENLEAF
BOOK GROUP PRESS

This book is intended as a reference volume only. It is sold with the understanding that the publisher and author are not engaged in rendering any professional services. The information given here is designed to help you make informed decisions. If you suspect that you have a problem that might require professional treatment or advice, you should seek competent help.

Published by Greenleaf Book Group Press
Austin, Texas
www.gbgpress.com

Distributed by Greenleaf Book Group

For ordering information or special discounts for bulk purchases, please contact Greenleaf Book Group at PO Box 91869, Austin, TX 78709, 512.891.6100.

Design and composition by Greenleaf Book Group
Cover design by Greenleaf Book Group

Publisher's Cataloging-in-Publication data is available.

Print ISBN: 979-8-88645-242-6

eBook ISBN: 979-8-88645-243-3

To offset the number of trees consumed in the printing of our books, Greenleaf donates a portion of the proceeds from each printing to the Arbor Day Foundation. Greenleaf Book Group has replaced over 50,000 trees since 2007.

Printed in the United States of America on acid-free paper

24 25 26 27 28 29 30   10 9 8 7 6 5 4 3 2 1

First Edition

CONTENTS

INTRODUCTION

I think my quest started around my twenties—the search-ing, the wondering, the hows, and the whys. From that age onward, I was a searcher; I meditated, sought fulfillment, and thought I could find it in relationships and travel, but I could never exactly pinpoint the cause of my uneasiness. Around the age of forty, I began to understand that there was something funda-mentally wrong. You could call me a late bloomer. At the time, I blamed my feelings of emptiness on my relationship. I felt trapped in my role as the sole provider for my family, with a husband who always seemed to know better and a wonderful child for whom I could not be the mother I wanted to be.

When my husband and I got a divorce, I regained my freedom, became the energetic mum who could raise her son the way she wanted to, and started pursuing my passions. Or so I thought. It turned out to be a fairy tale. My issues just weren't that simple.

Sure, I regained my freedom with the divorce, even though, because I was the breadwinner, I had to go into debt to meet my maintenance (alimony) obligations. I blossomed in my mother-hood—okay, part-time motherhood, because of the co-parenting agreement. After getting over the strange and unnatural feeling of not seeing my six-year-old son half of the time, I came to realize that I had no clue what I truly wanted from life. What passions did I have? I didn't know. What did I want to put all my energy into? The uneasy feeling of emptiness kept lingering. It didn't go away. It lay silently inside me, waiting to strike the moment I started thinking too much about life again.

To compensate for this feeling, I went into overdrive, devising plans to fill the hole inside me. I tried one dream after the other. One moment I wanted to completely immerse myself in painting, and the next, I fantasized about starting a meditation center. But every time I considered trying something new, I conjured up all kinds of objections, felt insecure about my direction, and doubted if it was worth the sacrifices. Was this what I wanted? I watched myself in amazement. I discovered that I didn't know myself as well as I thought. I didn't know what I truly wanted or what would give my life purpose.

Only one thing was certain: I wanted to take responsibility for my life and no longer blame the "external circumstances." I had to solve something inside myself, within myself. And even though I didn't know how to, my journey began.

A SECOND-CHOICE LIFE

During that search, I found that I had the tendency to live what I call a second-choice life—a life that had "befallen" me, that I hadn't consciously chosen, and in which I was simply floating around. I wasn't realizing my full potential, as I would in my first-choice life; I was simply adjusting to the circumstances. I wasn't following the path to what I truly wanted—actually, I couldn't even remember what I wanted. I was living a full-on second-choice life.

I stumbled upon the term "second-choice life" in a book: *The Secret of Hollywood.*[1] The book reveals the golden formula for the success of Hollywood movies: there is a problem; a main character who has to move from a second-choice life toward a first-choice life; and five plans (of which four fail) to get to that first-choice life. The problem is that the main character is living a second-choice life—one that doesn't reflect their true passions—but they find that hard to admit or realize. They prefer to stay in that safe and familiar second-choice life that is missing something, in which they are not fully happy. In this comfort zone, they can never realize their full potential unless they confront their deepest pain, trauma, or fear and change to move toward a first-choice life. In Hollywood movies, the main character always has to face such a problem so they have no choice but to change. For instance, Jack Nicholson's character in *As Good as It Gets* has to overcome his compulsive patterns or he will lose the woman he loves. Sylvester Stallone as Rocky must face his insecurities or he cannot prove himself to Adrian, the love of his life. In *Not Without My Daughter*, Sally Field's character must do everything she can to flee Iran or she loses her daughter.

Learning about this golden formula stirred up strong feelings in me. I felt as if I were watching the scenario of my own life being played out. I felt like crying and laughing at the same time. Like the main character in a movie, I had ended up in a second-choice life. I realized that I would lose myself if I didn't discover my passions and organize my life the way it was intended for me.

In movies, four out of five plans fail, to keep the movie interesting, but in real life, our attempts fail too. It's not easy to recognize that you're living a second-choice life and even less easy to get out of one. In this book, I will give you an insight into my failed plans, how my path toward a first-choice life became clear to me, and which steps I took to end up in a first-choice life.

HOW THIS BOOK WORKS

This book is meant for you if you feel that there is more to life, you feel empty, you don't feel fully happy, or you find yourself at the same crossroads over and over again and don't know which path to take. This book is for you if you want to live your full potential. I found some pieces of the puzzle and have put them all together in this narrative, through which I weave my personal life story to clarify the process I went through and the questions that may arise.

A mentor once told me: "Through the sharing of your experiences, you might accelerate the path of another." So, I hope my journey will inspire you! There's nothing better than living your full potential. It's an adventure, a journey you shouldn't be missing out on. And the world isn't complete without your unique contribution to it.

Part I

A SECOND-CHOICE LIFE STARTS UNNOTICED

Chapter 1

THE ELEVENTH COMMANDMENT

The Bible preaches ten commandments, and my parents added an eleventh one: "Thou shalt not air one's dirty linen in public." It was an unwritten, outspoken, and unspoken rule. From early childhood on, we were aware of it. This was how it should be, how it must be, just as coercive as the rules we learned in the Catholic Church.

As a child, I didn't fully understand the term "dirty linen," but I did understand the unspoken rule. Though no one in my family ever used the phrase, it so perfectly captures my family's mentality that I have adopted it as my unique spin to describe the prevalent attitude in our home. My brother had a phobia for water, and no one was allowed to talk about it. My mum was regularly ill, but to the outside world, I had to say that she was fine. My teacher in kindergarten put me in the corner because I was making race-car noises and was too exuberant—but that was no one's business; teachers only did nice things.

At my grandfather's house, the eleventh commandment also took on a physical form. We were not allowed in the parlor. What was said there was not meant for children. But being such a curious child, one day I decided to eavesdrop behind the sliding doors with the stained-glass windows. It didn't take long before I got caught. I couldn't see the adults through the stained glass, but they could see me because of my silhouette. The rest of that afternoon I had to sit on a chair in the kitchen as a punishment.

But what I found worse was that the girls in our family seemed to have more rules than the boys. We had to keep our clothes clean while the boys could come back home covered in mud. I found that unfair and difficult, as I loved climbing trees and building treehouses. But my mum didn't care about my reasoning. The eleventh commandment prevailed: Climb trees but keep your skirt clean and don't complain about the rules. Moreover, I regularly fell and ripped holes in my trousers. My mother would then, muttering, sew some fabric over the rip with an image of an apple or a pear on it. This resulted in schoolmates bastardizing my last name: "Rotteveel" became "rotting apple" or "rotting pear."

I got used to the fact that I shouldn't speak about what we were going through as a family, what we did, and how we treated each other. Luckily, I had a few good friends with whom I shared a lot, as well as a surrogate grandmother.

My two sisters and two brothers solemnly obeyed that eleventh commandment: "Thou shalt not air one's dirty linen in public." That's why no one asked me how I felt when I had to report to the police station at fifteen, and how that came to be (story to follow).

That was something we didn't talk about.

FISHY BUSINESS

Beginning in the sixth grade, I delivered leaflets (advertising brochures). Independence and self-reliance were considered important in our family. When I was thirteen, I secretly started smoking, went to the frat (our name for a community center for young people), and liked buying cool clothes. In those days, money meant freedom to me. I took a second leaflet delivery route, but after a year, I realized it didn't earn as much as I wanted. I heard there was good money in the fish business, so since school finished at one-thirty p.m. on Thursdays, I decided to start working in the harbor on Thursday afternoons. I knew the area well, loved the rowdiness of that world, wandered around there a lot, and knew which businesses were located where.

First, I started asking for work at the bigger businesses. "You're not fifteen yet; come back in six months," is what they told me. So I changed my strategy and started visiting the smaller businesses. After a few afternoons of asking, a fish-packing company took my bait and hired me. Floating on air, I walked back home through the park. I had done it! I had gotten the job! I was so happy with my new job. In just two Thursday afternoons, I could earn as much as a full month of delivering leaflets. And the work didn't seem that difficult. Shipments of frozen fish and frog legs arrived at the company in large containers, and I had to help pack them into handy cardboard boxes for wholesalers at home and abroad.

I thoroughly enjoyed my first afternoon at the packing center. The place buzzed with activity, and all that I saw amazed me.

continued

Against the rear wall of the large, rectangular space were the freezers with the containers of fish and frog legs. Men scooped up the creatures from the containers and transferred them into carts with trays. Those carts were pushed up to the assembly line where other workers packed the meat and sent the carts back empty. Along the walls perpendicular to the freezer cells were pallets with stacks of flat cardboard boxes. Two men continuously folded boxes and taped the bottoms. The conveyor belt commanded the attention in the center of the room.

The folded boxes formed the starting point of the continuously moving belt. The first woman at the conveyor belt put plastic in a box, her neighbor filled the box with the first layer of frog legs or fish, the woman next to her packed in the next layer, and so on, until the box was full. The second-to-last woman folded the plastic and the box at the top, and the last one taped it shut.

From there, men stacked the boxes on pallets and then drove the full pallets with a forklift to the freezer cells on the other side. Everyone had their own task, everything was coordinated, and meanwhile, there was a lot of laughter, shouting, and cursing if something went wrong.

As the shortest worker, I stood on a box at the conveyor belt between the stout women in their twenties and thirties. With large rubber gloves, I grabbed the fish from the tanks on the cart behind us and lined them up neatly in the box. I enjoyed my female coworkers. With their shrill voices, they made jokes about men, chatted about getting perms, which hair dyes were the best, and about the invention of the tampon. The latter was new to me. At home, we used fabric sanitary pads, and if I went out dancing,

I used disposable ones. The women roared with laughter; they couldn't imagine it, a tight pair of trousers and then a big ball of sanitary pads between your thighs. Better than a scary thing deep in your vagina, I thought.

The women were not easily embarrassed; they told each other all about their love lives and shared openly about their sorrows. As a girl raised in a strict Catholic home, my ears were always open, and I eagerly absorbed all their stories.

Now and then, I was assigned as taper of the boxes, last in line at the conveyor belt. On such days, I worked with a giant of a man nicknamed Goliath who stacked the full boxes on the pallets. He liked to talk to himself, and I was a bit scared of him. According to my colleagues, there was no need for that; he was a little eccentric but incredibly kind.

Among the men and the women at the center, a lot of flirting took place during the workday. Hearing playful verbal jabs and seeing airborne empty boxes was common. It didn't seem to bother anyone much if a box or two got torn in the process.

Even our boss—always dressed in a beige suit with a tie—was fine with most things as long as the daily output was reached. Daily at eleven a.m. and four p.m., he checked our progress and counted the pallets. He wore a big gold-colored watch around his wrist, which my colleagues insisted was a genuine Rolex. If we were behind schedule, he held up his Rolex and tapped on it. "Hurry up, boys and girls, otherwise you'll have to stay over late," he'd declare. The daily output was sacred to him, and nobody even dared to think of going home before it was achieved.

continued

The moments of inspection were the only times I saw the big boss. I rather liked him; he never said anything to me, but he always smiled in a friendly manner. His son, however, the second boss who had hired me, remained a mysterious figure. He never showed his face at the packing center, and because the sales room and the packing room had separate entrances, I hadn't seen him after the job interview. Only by his silver Mercedes could I see that he was there.

~~~

I was paid by the hour, and after a few months I expanded my working hours from Thursday afternoons to other hours that had been dropped at school due to sick teachers. I even started skipping school at some point because the packing earned me good money. I really enjoyed myself at the packing center, and I was proud to receive an invitation to the Christmas party; it made me feel a sense of complete belonging there.

For the occasion, the center was thoroughly tidied up and cleaned. Along the wall where the pallets with cardboard boxes normally stood was now a long drinks table with a beer tap, bottles of wine, and heartier liquors to mix with soft drinks. And another long table displayed snacks. The conveyor belt had been pushed aside, and in its place stood cheerful bar tables with Christmassy centerpieces on top. Father and son each gave a short speech, we raised a glass to us and the past year, and then the Christmas party really commenced.

My female colleagues were barely recognizable in their tight dresses and painted lips, and they laughed a lot and aloud. The boss's son had a similar watch as his father. It swished back and forth when he walked, so I had to stare at it. Both he and his father were popular among the women and men of the packing center. Other colleagues from the office, whom I didn't know, were also in attendance. Goliath, the blond giant, stood in the middle of their group, and nobody seemed to notice me. I liked that.

Awkwardly sipping from my 7UP with berry gin, I nonchalantly leaned against the wall. The pace of drinking accelerated, and the atmosphere grew louder by the minute. The blond giant had enough of the people laughing at him and left the group, making his way over to stand next to me. I only reached up to his belly button and looked up tentatively.

"They are already quite drunk, aren't they?" I said, just to make conversation.

He nodded. "You'd better go home."

Surprised, I looked up at him. I had never heard him speak so clearly. "Any fun plans for Christmas?" I asked.

The giant grumbled, rubbed his upper lip against his nose, and moved it back and forth. He then bowed down to me. "You, nice girl, go home."

I had nothing else I'd rather do, it wasn't even five o'clock yet, and I thought it would be rude to go home already. Two colleagues were shamelessly kissing each other against the freezer cells. In the group in the middle, a colleague got angry and started to give out some blows. One of my female colleagues tried to pull the hitting colleague back by his shirt. She was pushed over and fell on the floor, screaming. The big boss intervened and the row was over. Drinks were topped off and the party continued happily. I was used

continued

to the frat and the local pub; heavy drinking was commonplace there too. But this, so early in the day—the giant was right. It was time to go.

"Okay, I'll just say goodbye, and then I'll leave."

He snorted contently and mumbled to himself. I walked over to the big boss to thank him for the Christmas party.

"I'll walk with you," he said. "We have a Christmas box for you."

I almost burst with pride. I was getting a Christmas box. Delighted, I looked up at him. "Thank you so much!"

"Come on." He pulled me by my arm. "They're in the hall near the office."

"See you next year!" I yelled and waved to my colleagues, and I followed my boss.

The Christmas boxes were stacked neatly in the hallway. I ran my finger over the boxes and surely, there was a box with my name on it.

"You're happy with that, aren't you?" my boss said.

"So happy!" I replied. If only he knew. My first Christmas box. Only meant for me. I smiled at him, and my boss was visibly pleased that I was so happy with it.

"Maybe I can get a little kiss from you," he said. He came closer to me with his sweaty body and locked me in between the wall and the boxes.

"Uhm, I have to go home."

"A little kiss wouldn't be a problem, would it?" And without waiting for my reply, he pressed his fleshy wet lips on mine.

I felt startled and struggled to get out of the boxes. Suddenly, there stood the giant. He picked my boss up as if he were light as a feather and put him away in the office. Next, he pulled me out-side, and we ran off the grounds, around the fence, and across the street, until we reached the woods. Panting, we fell on our hands and knees in the bushes. My head was pounding. The giant mum-bled and mumbled. We heard screams coming from inside the building. Carefully, I looked through the branches to see if I could see anything, but it was already dark outside.

Car engines started, and headlights illuminated the area. Slowly, the Mercedes and other cars were circling the fences of the building. I anxiously gripped Goliath's arm.

"They're looking for us," I whispered.

He grumbled, and I thought I saw his lips move back and forth. We retreated a little bit more into the bushes and tried to make ourselves invisible. One of the cars slowly moved toward the bushes, and the headlights of the search car brushed right past us. The giant panted but didn't move. The car moved on. Another car drove past the bushes. This one stopped, and I clawed my nails into the ground. Someone got out of the car and started pushing away the branches while walking past the bushes. I held my breath. The giant had stopped panting. Not until the man got back into the car did I release my breath. Frozen, I watched as the car slowly drove away. It was winter and cold, but I could feel the sweat dripping down my back. After a few more laps, the search cars drove away to the harbor, farther away from the packaging company.

"Now go home," the giant said, and with his big hands he put me back on my feet.

I was trembling.

continued

"Go," he said with urgency. "They'll be back shortly."

I nodded in the dark and made my way through the bushes toward the street. The whole way back home, I was running, seeking cover against trees, fences, and walls.

When I got home, my mum was cooking dinner in the kitchen.

"I'm back!" I yelled and quickly disappeared into my room.

At the sink, I scrubbed my hands clean and splashed some water on my face. I looked at my reflection in the mirror; no one could tell that something bad had happened. In my little attic room, I lay down on my bed and tried to control my body's trembling. Tears welled up in my eyes, and I clenched my fists, fighting back the urge to cry. "Don't cry," I told myself.

I shifted my focus to the poster of Starsky and Hutch that adorned the slanted ceiling. Starsky was my hero. I fantasized how he would rescue me, hitting my boss in the face, and how we would drive off in his red car, leaving the search cars behind in a cloud of dust. I hadn't even thanked the giant.

Half an hour later, I was called downstairs for dinner. Thankfully, dinner never took long at our house. My mum would always cook for an hour or more, but within fifteen minutes, the food was devoured. Saying the Lord's Prayer at the start of the meal almost took longer than eating the meal itself.

Nobody asked me questions about the Christmas party; no one seemed to notice anything unusual about me. But when we were clearing the table, the phone rang and my father picked up.

"They are expecting you at the police station," my father said as he hung up the phone.

"Why?" I asked.

"It seems that you know why."

"I didn't do anything."

He stared at me with a dark look in his eyes. "They arrested someone, and you've got something to do with it. They want to question you."

Question me. I envisioned a neon-lit room, a rectangular table, and two detectives in front of me who didn't believe me. "I swear, I didn't do anything."

"I told them you're on your way," he said brusquely.

My oldest brother came to my rescue. "I'll go with you," he said.

~~~~~

At the police station, they referred us to two officers in uniform. They took us to a room—neon lit, yes, but somehow less threatening than on TV. They told me the giant had been taken into custody because my boss thought he had kidnapped me. I couldn't believe it. I explained to them that it couldn't be further from the truth, that my boss had tried to kiss me. The officers looked at each other.

"Are you sure about that?" the tallest of the two asked.

Of course, I was sure about that. I told them about how the giant and I had fled the building, about how we hid in the bushes, and about the search cars.

The officers took notes and replied every now and then with okay, yes, and what happened next? Finally, the tallest asked me how much I had to drink. "Half a glass of 7UP with berry gin." They now knew enough, and we were asked to wait in the hallway.

I was close to breaking down in tears. I hadn't even thanked the giant, and now he was stuck behind bars. I couldn't make any

continued

sense out of it. My brother sat quietly next to me. It was sweet of him to come along with me.

Soon after, the officers returned. The tallest told us that the giant would be released and we could go home.

"Are you going to do something about my boss?" I asked the officer.

He shook his head. "This is a tempest in a teapot," he said. "That's our final conclusion."

Back home, my brother said: "It was nothing. Just a tempest in a teapot."

"Well done," my father said to my brother. He couldn't even look me in the eye. My mum did but didn't say anything. *Why can't you behave yourself for once?* I could hear her think.

I went upstairs to my little attic room and lay down on my bed. I stared at the Starsky and Hutch poster again, wishing I hadn't gone to that stupid Christmas party. My body started trembling again. I didn't want to cry. I just wanted to leave this whole incident behind as soon as possible.

This was a crucial moment in my life. I was confused and in shock, I felt guilty, and all sorts of emotions were mixing together. Weeks after the incident, I could still feel his lips on mine. And yet, I never told my best friends about it. Nothing at all. Even worse: I lied to them. I told them that I'd gotten tired of working in the fish business, even though it was very lucrative.

I obeyed the eleventh commandment within our family, but also outside of our family. By keeping silent, by not airing my dirty linen in public, I pushed a massive rock into the stream of my life. It became the start of a dam.

~~~

My boss contacted me after New Year's Eve and apologized for his behavior. In hindsight, he understood that his little kiss had startled me. "Too much booze and not enough to eat, it will never happen again," he promised. He asked me if I wanted to work for him again, but I declined. I was fifteen now and able to work at other companies at the harbor.

Unfortunately, I had told my friends I was tired of working in the fish business. I hadn't thought this excuse through well enough. And I was accustomed to spending money, so I urgently needed another job. I found one at a butchery as a shopgirl. Working for a whole Saturday earned me just enough for cigarettes and the frat. Now bringing in far less money, I had to change my lifestyle drastically—no more nice clothes and extras like chips and cookies—but I preferred that over airing out my dirty linen and confessing to my lie.

Looking back now, I see that that was the moment I unknowingly got caught in a second-choice life. I had surrendered, accepted the unwritten rules without questioning them, believed that I was the one who had put myself in a dangerous situation, that I was the only one to blame for it, and agreed that one shouldn't talk about this with others.

Until that day, I had shared everything with my best friends. But now I kept silent and lied to them. At the time, I didn't understand that keeping silent about such an important event created a distance between my friends and me, that keeping silent didn't mean the event would go away.

I also lied to myself. I told myself that I should not talk about it, that it was best to try and forget this whole situation as soon as possible. I convinced myself I was lucky that I had a job at the butchery, even though the earnings were poor and I missed my loud colleagues.

My parents never spoke about it again, and neither did I. The dirty linen is neither aired out in public nor within the family. The dirty linen is thrown in the cellar. That's where it's safe, in the dark, rotting. The door is securely locked so no one can smell it.

Have you ever been through an event in your childhood that you'd rather not talk about or prefer to lie about? What impact did this event have on your life?

Chapter 2

UNSEEN: THE SYMPTOMS OF A SECOND-CHOICE LIFE

We do often notice that something is missing from our lives. Intuitively, we know we are not completely fulfilling our dreams and wishes, but we cannot pinpoint the issue exactly. Signs that indicate a second-choice life are often ignored, overlooked, or misunderstood.

What a joy it would have been if I had recognized the warning signs on my path as being symptoms of a second-choice life. Because to step out of a second-choice life, you have to know that you're living one. But what are the signs? I will explain them shortly. Maybe you'll recognize a few too.

NEVERLAND, AN ESCAPE

Michael Jackson created a whole new world on his estate, Neverland, a Peter Pan estate where he was master and commander and the outside world couldn't harm him, where he could escape reality.

We all need some escape from reality from time to time. I love burying myself in a good book, laughing at a comedy on TV, or being transported into a character's adventures in a movie. But if we feel caught in a second-choice life, we might feel tempted to escape too often in our own world as a substitute for engaging in reality—in books, movies, sports, our jobs, or whatever. And with that, we reinforce our second-choice life.

BOOKS AND A CHESTNUT TREE

After the incident at the fish packaging company, I went through a difficult time. I had lied to my friends and started avoiding them. At home, I tried to make myself invisible. I kept wondering if my parents were, in fact, my real parents. I felt that real parents should have somehow cared more.

I devoured books by Daphne du Maurier and Isabel Allende. Both authors write about mysticism, secrets, and relationships. I was transported into those worlds. I started seeing intrigue all around me and developed a strong imagination as I associated myself with the characters from my books. As I turned more inward and sought silence, I even became more receptive to the energies surrounding us, such as a tree's aura. My best friends in those days were my dog, with whom I roamed through the dunes for hours, and the tall chestnut tree at the park, which patiently watched over me.

When I'm writing this down, it sounds like this was a dark period in my life, but it didn't feel like that back then. I was living in my own world, which was enough for me. The most difficult thing during that time was to keep being part of school, our family, and my friends. We were drifting apart. I felt like I was looking at the people around me through a glass door. I couldn't reach them or touch them. They could see me, but then again, they could not. Real contact was impossible. I preferred to bury myself in my books, roam around with my dog, or feel secure with the chestnut tree at the park.

This hazy time in my life lasted only a few months, and like everything else, it passed. I met new people who knew nothing about me, and over time, the fishy incident faded into the background, which helped me be more open with my friends again.

These "Neverland episodes" repeated themselves later in life. Second-choice and first-choice lives alternated, and the more the unconscious unease about my second-choice life began to increase, the more I buried myself in my books, roamed around in the dunes, and turned inward. In hindsight, those were the most recognizable signs of a second-choice life for me.

Naturally, I still enjoy a good book or roaming around the dunes in my first-choice life, but I felt different during those Neverland episodes; I was seeking refuge. Escape wasn't a free choice but *necessary* to keep my life going. In those times, when I was walking in the dunes, I could feel the air in my lungs, and I could breathe again. I walked and read, not to feel my subdued unrest but to seek refuge in something. You can recognize an unhealthy escape in yourself when you are being too fanatical, too fixated, too much, having to, or absolutely needing to.

~~~

I am grateful for that period of seeking refuge and turning inward after the fishy incident. Later, I knew that I could visit my Neverland as a reliable state of being, and I could also come out of it. I was the one who largely created that feeling of absence and not being understood.

When people don't feel understood because they feel different, I always think back to that time when I was hypersensitive and emotionally turned inward. To this day, I still can feel certain energies stemming from that time. And like everyone else, I still have times when I don't feel understood. But now I have learned that being understood by others is only partially possible, in the same way we also can't fully understand others, even though it sometimes seems like we do. We can't read each other's minds or feel exactly what the other person feels.

And if we are living a second-choice life, we are, per definition, closed off from others and from ourselves. We have built dams in our streams of life, and in those murky stagnant waters, we don't see clearly. We don't live to our full potential. In a second-choice life, being different is not the problem. It's being closed off—the not living our full potential—that causes the problem. Our own Neverland is an alluring and safe place, but it's not the same as our home.

Neverland: are your hobbies, job, books, and movies an escape, or are they healthy tools for relaxation?

NOT KNOWING WHAT YOU TRULY WANT

In my teens, everything I actually wanted went out the window. As a child, I had been taught that the idea was not to follow my heart but to do what was expected of me. During my teen years, I would still generally do what was expected but with a reluctant stubbornness. That stubbornness seemed the only thing I could hold onto to not lose myself completely.

FIGHTING WITH MY DAD

After the fish packaging company incident, I started working on Saturdays at the butchery. Meanwhile, I was in my fourth year in high school, and that meant I had to start asking myself what I wanted to do after school. I wanted to be a stewardess—to travel, to get far away from home, to see the world, and to get to know other cultures. That was my dream. The only problem was my height; to become a stewardess, you had to be five foot three, and I was only five feet tall.

Discrimination, I wrote to the Dutch airline KLM.

This height requirement was necessary to be able to open and close the storage lockers in the airplane, they wrote back.

There was nothing I could do about it, so I tried my best to grow. When I stood upright, I tried to look taller by stretching myself as much as possible. I ate more vegetables, and at night, I promised myself that I would have grown another inch in the morning. Every week, I took my measurements. But I only grew a half inch in a few months. I kept encouraging myself, but the voice in my head that

continued

said I would never be able to reach that preferable height started to become louder and louder. I needed a plan B.

The internet didn't exist in those days, and at school, we only received basic information about job possibilities. But at the library, I found some folders with lists of colleges; in one of those folders, I found the College for Tourism in Breda, Netherlands. That sounded amazing! A college for tourism. And I had all the credentials to be accepted; maybe plan B was even better than plan A: tourism, an internship abroad, and in the future, a job abroad as well. And the location of the college was a bonus for me. I could spend weekdays in my own room with a landlady, and on the weekends, I could go home. Or maybe I wouldn't go home at all. Suddenly, life seemed good again. Enthusiastically, I told my dad about the plan.

"College?" he said. "Absolutely not. After finishing school, you'll get a job, just like your sister and your brothers. Going to Breda . . ." He polished his glasses and put them back on his nose. "What were you thinking?" End of conversation.

I tried asking my mother. "You heard your father," she replied.

I wasn't aware that there were scholarships available to fund my studies, and after this conversation with my parents, I lost interest in school completely. There was no point in studying if I couldn't further my education, so I stopped looking for a plan C. If I had to get a job, I'd rather start immediately. I turned sixteen in May, and the following summer, I quit school.

My father and I got into a fight about that. He didn't want me to leave school without a diploma. You can't work at good companies without a diploma, like the National Postal and Telephone Service, where my sister worked, or the Royal Steelworks, where he worked. Good employers, where you could work for the rest of your life, had become his ideal after he quit his flower-bulb business ten years earlier. At the climax of our fight, we came to a deal. I could get a job if I got my high school diploma in night school. To me, money still meant freedom, so I was satisfied.

I exchanged my Saturday job at the butchery for a full-time job at another butchery in a supermarket, then one in a gas station, and after that a bakery. All were extremely dull jobs. Meanwhile, I got my diploma, and my father turned out to be right. With my diploma, I transferred from store jobs to office jobs. I became a typist at the municipality (a government job), and with that job, I suddenly earned one and a half times as much as I had before.

A second bonus was that my colleagues were lovely women who were right at the heart of life and just as open as the women I had worked with at the fish packaging company. Together with the ushers and the reproduction department, we were the lowest in rank in the municipality, which provided us with a sense of unity. It felt like home, and those days were carefree. I spent most of my salary on partying, clothes, and my scooter. My father sputtered shortly that I should save up, but with the fight about school still fresh in our minds, we made a kind of truce.

That truce, however, didn't mean there was peace at my house. On the contrary, a new and intense conflict rose up unexpectedly, and with great force. A male colleague at my father's work turned out to be gay, and he had a "coming out." My dad despised gay people, and so did the Catholic Church. I thought it was really cool that someone was brave enough to come out and that more people should do so. The truce faltered.

continued

"Don't say such foolish things," my dad said. "Homosexuality doesn't do anyone any good."

"Neither does the church."

The battle commenced. My dad forbade me to talk about gay people or "coming out" at home. I didn't let that slide and started asking him questions about his colleague. Did he start wearing different clothes? How did his family feel about it? What was the reaction of his other colleagues? My father didn't respond and turned on his chess computer. But I was out for war and took it up a notch. I asked how he would respond if I came out. Maybe I was a lesbian.

He put his chess computer aside and rose up in front of me. "You have a boyfriend, and I don't want to hear these things in my house. Now, stop it."

But I was out for blood. "Your colleague is married to a woman. So it doesn't mean anything that I have a boyfriend."

"Stop it!" he said. "And if you can't do that, then maybe you don't belong here."

Then I don't belong here, went through my mind. I fell silent and stared at the sansevierias—plants with narrow, stiff, straight leaves that can withstand anything—on the windowsill. These plants can endure little water, a lot of water, direct sunlight, and the dark. Our windowsill was full of them because those plants were so easy to maintain.

I was not such a plant. I didn't belong here. The sentence kept repeating in my head, over and over again. *I don't belong here. I don't belong here.*

My father sat down again, with his feet on the footstool and his chess computer on his lap. When I was ten, he taught me how to play chess. But I had quit playing because I had never been able to beat him. He also beat the computer most of the time, but that thing couldn't quit and had to continue playing until my father had had enough. I didn't want that anymore, the feeling that someone else wanted to control my thoughts, my behavior, what I could and couldn't do, programmed like a computer.

"Then I don't belong here," I said.

My father didn't respond.

"Then I don't belong here," I said again.

My father moved his knight, and a pawn had to clear the field. With the pawn in his hand, he looked up at me. "Why is it always so difficult for you to behave yourself?"

~~~

The battle had been fought. Within two weeks, I had found a place to live. Not in IJmuiden, but in Haarlem, in a high street over an office. The landlord didn't know what kind of office it was, and it didn't say on the facade either, but whatever they were doing behind those closed blinds, I didn't care.

Behind a shared front door, a small hall led to a steep staircase to a small landing on the first floor. Here, there were two doors and another staircase leading up. The first door gave access to the toilet and shower that I had to share with the upstairs neighbor, a moldy space measuring 3 X 5 feet. The other door was the door to the room that was available to let. It was a large, long room with high front and back windows. The walls were covered with yellowish woodchip wallpaper, and a bright blue kitchen unit was in the back left corner.

continued

I immediately fell in love with the large tree that stood behind the property. Its branches reached for the back window, as if it were making a welcoming bow to me. In that same window, two large cracks were fixed with sticky tape. According to the landlord, it had been like that for years, and it was sturdy as anything. The room was available immediately, and I said yes. I loved it. Life could begin, and I was finally free! I could do whatever I wanted. Say whatever I wanted. Go my own way, with no commandments, limitations, written and unwritten rules ever again. Freedom. At the time, I really thought that. But that "the world is your oyster" feeling didn't stick for too long.

Because, of course, life turned out differently. What did I know? I had no idea how to live my own life. Now, at only seventeen years old, I had only been taught how to navigate between the eleven commandments, how to survive a strict Catholic school, and how to stay silent. And I had a boyfriend—a tall, quiet boy I knew from work. He was kind and caring, and his parents were nice. Not that they spoke a lot about life at his house, about what kept you busy, about your dreams, but they also didn't keep quiet about it. My boyfriend offered to come and live with me, and without giving it another thought, without asking myself if that was something I wanted, we moved in together.

And that's how I suddenly found myself living with my boyfriend. It just went that way. I had no desire to move in together; I just wanted to leave my parental home.

With my decision to leave home, I briefly disrupted my second-choice life. I demanded space for my own life, my own thoughts, and my own expressive power. In doing so, albeit unintentionally, I entered the current of the source, the current of a first-choice life.

The source, the soul, the impersonal self, the God within ourselves—there are many words for something that cannot be described. For me, the word "source" resonates the most.

Source: a calm, vibrating energy that is always present; an energy that cannot be distorted. Thoughts, emotions, and our body can distort that which wants to manifest itself through us, but the pulsating energy of the source remains imperturbable. The source is always at our disposal.

Despite the housing shortage, I had managed to find a place to live. However, I lacked the knowledge of how to sustain that sense of flow, of living in harmony with the source, the pure energy that provides us with everything we require.

All we need to do is connect our minds, emotions, and intuition. In fact, we all know the source. Art can touch us deeply. If it's created from the source, it strikes a chord. We are being drawn into the artwork, as it were. Music does this. A sunrise or a sunset can do it. Sailing on a vast blue sea can give me that feeling. I look at the glistening water, and suddenly, there is only water. Hours pass without my realization when I'm writing my book. I lose myself in it; it flows out of me without my personal interference.

But as a seventeen-year-old, I didn't know anything about the source, let alone understand how it worked. At the time, it only made sense to move into that room together. Financially, it would have been hard for me without the support of my boyfriend. I liked him a lot, and his family stood behind us.

It was just that I had no clue what I wanted from life at that time. I only knew what I *didn't* want.

Throughout my life, I have noticed that not knowing what you want, not knowing where your passions lie, and not knowing what makes you want to get up in the morning (aside from your partner, your family, or your job) is a strong indication of a second-choice life. I had received those signs multiple times in my life and ignored them—every time for a different reason.

Looking back, the "not knowing what I wanted" was a recurring theme in my life. I let others decide what was best for me. I allowed career tests, advice from my partners, friends, opportunism, and external circumstances to decide. I simply followed their orders because I hadn't clarified for myself what I wanted.

Nowadays, I have learned that the moment I let others make decisions for me, the answers will never be mine. Getting advice always led to me going along with other people's thoughts, which meant that I let others make decisions for me. In those moments, I didn't follow my own ideas and wishes enough, resulting in a life that had little to do with who I was. It turned into a superficial life that met social norms and the approval of those around me. I desperately wanted to believe that this was the right direction for me. And, of course, everyone meant well. I wasn't unhappy. But in following those good intentions, I got stuck in a second-choice life. And ultimately, that isn't good enough.

Do you always know what you want? If not, how do you come to a decision? If you do, is this really what you want, or is it based on an idea from the people around you?

NOT-FOR-ME

The human mind often likes to play with the concept of "not-for-me," usually in a negative but also in a positive sense. For example, we can look at other people with admiration; these people do something that we would also like to do or achieve, yet we don't even try because we tell ourselves this is not-for-me. We come up with various reasons: these people have wealthy parents, are better educated, are more talented, don't have the same fears as us, and so on. On the positive side, we can also be happy that something is not-for-me because it means we are doing better than the other person.

But negatively or positively, is what that little voice in our head telling us true? That is something we should ask ourselves more often. And like death, not-for-me comes in various guises.

The "Not-the-Right-Circumstances-for-Me"

As a child, I got to know *not-the-right-circumstances-for-me* for the first time. Someone did something that lit a fire in me (story to follow). Suddenly, I was wide awake. I felt myself come to life. I was inspired. But I immediately doused that fire; I concluded that my circumstances didn't allow me to follow that passion.

THE SICK GIRL

As a child, the library was heaven on earth. I read about all kinds of things. Books unlocked a world where I could travel to far-off

continued

countries, get to know new cultures, and learn how other families behaved at home.

One time, I read a book about a twelve-year-old girl, a little older than I was at that time, who told all about her experiences at a sanatorium. She lived in Valkenburg, in the south of the Netherlands, suffered from tuberculosis, and was seriously ill. For her recovery, she was admitted to a sanatorium, far away from her family, in the middle of the woods, where squirrels ran over her bed. In those days, clean air and full bed rest formed the cure for tuberculosis.

The girl went through a difficult but beautiful time in that sanatorium. Spending whole days in bed was hard. The boredom and the homesickness were tough to bear. Another girl on her floor passed away. But she also had a lot of fun with the other patients; she was brave enough to stand up to the head nurse, and she received stamps, postcards, and letters from all over the country after she placed an advertisement for her stamp collection in the newspaper. I loved the way she described the characters of the girls, the boys, and the nurses. And how she never sold herself short.

This book, *Blijf Lachen, Irmgard* (*Keep on Smiling, Irmgard*),[1] awoke something inside me. A spark—no, rather a fire of inspiration. How I wished I could write a book about what I was going through. I prayed to Mister Owl (the big stuffed owl that stood in my room, my mascot) that I would get as sick as the little girl and have to be admitted to a faraway place so I could write a book about it. I was extremely jealous of the sick girl.

In those days, I also kept a journal, but every two or three days, I ripped out the pages and burned them. If I had written something that I thought was overstepping the eleventh commandment,

I sometimes ripped out the page that same day, fearing that my mum would find my journal.

I felt that the circumstances were inexorable: writing a book was not-for-me.

The "Not-for-Me Comparison"

I frequently encountered the not-for-me in another guise, the guise of the comparison. I compared myself regularly with others. As a child, I already did that, both positively and negatively.

The eleventh commandment and everything that derived from it was quite difficult: you can't say that, we don't do that, you have to behave like this. But the upside was that my parents never asked me what I got up to after school. I could roam for hours along the harbor, climb forbidden fences, walk the dog along the canal, discover the bunkers in the dunes, and take the ferry up and down the water without anyone saying something about it.

My friends' parents, however, always wanted to know what we were up to and what we had been doing. So, in the *not-for-me comparison*, I thought my family did well. I couldn't have known then that showing interest in each other and sharing your whereabouts, your do's and don'ts, might actually be something invaluable.

In those days, I considered the *not-for-me comparison* as something positive. The sensation of freedom, that I could do whatever I wanted after school without anyone questioning me, was worth more to me than the eleventh commandment. That made me think I was better off with my family than most friends were with theirs.

The *not-for-me comparison* also worked the other way around. In those instances, I assessed my situation as negative compared to others.

THE TALL, QUIET BOY

Living together with the tall, quiet boy started off well. I really wanted to travel, and he had a car. We bought a small tent, took the ferry to Norway, and traveled around for almost five weeks. We had an amazing trip, adventure, and new encounters. By traveling, I had taken my first step on my new path.

But after a year, the monotony set in. Going out clubbing with my friends was over. I lost contact with my best friend from IJmuiden. I missed her. She often complained that I didn't have enough time for her and always put my boyfriend first. That was true because I didn't know how to navigate between the two. But I didn't tell her that.

The tall, quiet boy and I turned out to get along very well, even twenty-four hours a day. We lived together in harmony. And without questioning myself or the world around me, I went to work every day at the municipality. No freedom, no new life could start now; I started to adapt slowly to my surroundings. Our first trip remained our only trip; we saved up, moved to a nice flat in IJmuiden, and got ourselves a bunny.

Shortly before the move from the room to the flat, the tree broke the back window after a storm. Pieces of glass held on for dear life on the sticky tape, the tape that had been there for years. The tree had called me, but I didn't understand its message. Unknowingly, I had slipped into a second-choice life again.

Life carried on, until I fell head over heels in love with my motorcycle instructor. He was twice my age, married, and had kids. But unlike me, he was tough and free. And he had noticed me, too, and found me interesting and attractive. I kept quiet at home and made up all kinds of excuses to be able to go to our secret meetings.

The tall, quiet boy didn't notice anything; the women from the typing pool, however, did. They thought I was a bit withdrawn and kept bothering me until I told them what was going on. Eventually, I broke down and told them all about my predictable life, about how confused I was, how I didn't know what to expect from life or what I wanted from it, how I felt trapped in a relationship with a kind man, but it didn't sparkle. Not like the sparkle I felt when I was with the motorcycle instructor.

Those women loved me, and all of them recognized that feeling. They urged me to think carefully before making a change. All relationships have their ups and downs.

According to them, a relationship couldn't be exciting forever. One of the ladies went on holiday and let me stay at her apartment—to be alone, to think.

The tall, quiet boy felt uncomfortable about the fact that I was staying over at my colleague's flat for a week, but he had been noticing other strange things with my behavior.

continued

Spending that week alone did me good, and I decided to end the relationship. This time, the *not-for-me comparison* had negative consequences. My relationship with the tall, quiet boy was too calm compared to the relationships I had seen around me and even what I felt for that motorcycle instructor. But now was the time to rip off the Band-Aid.

"What do your colleagues make of this?" The tall, quiet boy hadn't seen it coming and didn't understand at all. For him, life was perfect with me. In comparison to others, we had everything we needed. There was a housing shortage, and we lived in a lovely rented flat. We were saving up to buy a house, and in the future, we could think about having children.

I was embarrassed that I wasn't the person he thought I was.

"You couldn't have thought of this six months ago?" he asked me after a while. The move to the flat in IJmuiden bothered him the most. Without me, he would have preferred to live in another flat in Haarlem, where his family lived.

I thought of the tree behind our old flat; it should have hit me over the head instead of only the window; maybe that would have helped. But unconsciously, I had continued our family tradition. No dirty linen outside. No dirty linen inside. My cellar became fuller and fuller, but the door could still close behind me. I left my tall, quiet boy with all our stuff and the sansevierias.

Because the *not-for-me comparison* is sometimes positive and sometimes negative, I like to see it as a seesaw. One moment, you're on top (positive). The next, you're down on the ground (negative). Up, down. Up, down. This will continue as long as you stay on that seesaw.

One moment in my life, I thought I wasn't doing so bad. The next, I saw other people chasing their dreams, going for it whatever the consequences. I compared myself with them, but I always drew the shorter straw. At work, I saw people with real talent, but it remained unclear if I was one of those people. They were smarter, they had their degrees. They had had a better start in life—and lots more of those thoughts.

The *not-for-me comparison* is a clear sign of a second-choice life. We diminish ourselves. We diminish our talents. Or we keep saying that we have everything we need in our lives without questioning if this is really the life that belongs to us and if we are truly living according to our passions. Either way, comparing yourself to others doesn't serve you, neither in a positive nor in a negative way. Comparisons can lead to feelings of superiority and inferiority. And both keep us from our true being. However, I only learned that after I restored the connection with my source.

I experienced periods in which I unknowingly was using the *not-for-me comparison*. I preferred being in denial about the fact that there were other possibilities instead of standing up for my passions.

The not-for-me seesaw felt safe. Because if we have to stand up for our passions and dreams, if we want to grow and develop our talents, there is a risk we could fail, too. If we talk about our desires out loud, people may think we're crazy, and they can ridicule us. Or, in my case, the eleventh commandment could put me back in my place. Realizing that showing up for myself was okay was something I had to learn.

Not-for-me comes in various guises. We might believe that everything is going fine in our lives until the moment we realize that we lack a particular talent or that our circumstances don't permit us to pursue that talent. Not-for-me serves as a potent indicator of a second-choice life because, more often than not, such thinking doesn't align with reality; we're essentially deceiving ourselves. If we embrace these false not-for-me notions, we are, in essence, surrendering before the battle even begins.

Have you ever found yourself on the not-for-me seesaw?

Which side do you prefer? Up: you boast to yourself and others that everything is great in your life; or down: other people are smarter or more talented.

AN INEXPLICABLE VOID

If I die tomorrow, would I be satisfied with the life I have lived so far? What is the purpose of life anyway? Those are some tough questions that I don't always want to think about.

Those questions can feel overwhelming when we are not connected to our source. The answers can cause sadness, unrest, loss of purpose, despair, and helplessness—a mixture of emotions that tends to gnaw at your soul, usually under the surface. I can feel the dissatisfaction when I walk alone through the woods, when I lie awake at night, or when I drive home in my car. And if I don't pay attention to it, it will only get worse. It feels like my soul is slowly dying.

THE POETIC AND PIANO-PLAYING TEACHER

After I had left my tall, quiet boyfriend with all our stuff and the san-sevierias, I was luckily able to move into a tiny room through my colleague at the municipality. Her father owned a house in Haarlem where she lived with her boyfriend, and the other two rooms were rentals. The room in the attic had just become available. With bags full of clothes strapped to the back of my bike, I moved from IJmuiden back to Haarlem.

My circle of friends had already gotten much smaller over the past three years, and now, after the breakup with the tall, quiet boy, I had nobody left. The motorcycle instructor had also bailed. The fact that I wasn't with my boyfriend anymore had made things difficult, according to him. In my tiny attic room, I sobbed uncontrollably as I stared out from my dormer window over the gardens and roofs of the houses behind ours. I bought a small fern. "What's the purpose of life?" I asked the fern. The plant unrolled its leaves from a curl. I often talked to it.

After a couple of weeks, the house turned out to be quite comfortable, and I connected with the girl who was renting the other room. I also booked myself an alpine lodge hike in Austria. It would be a challenging trip with a glacier crossing, snowfields, and climbing several mountain peaks with ropes and a guide. Adventure and hardship would do me good. The rugged outdoors had always helped me recharge; as a child, I loved hiking in the mountains. I had no need to think about the purpose of life for a while. I started living again.

continued

I took the bus from the Netherlands to Austria by myself and checked in at the guesthouse where we would depart with the group. Being only nineteen years old, I turned out to be the youngest and shortest. The tour guide asked me if I had prepared myself enough because, besides our backpacks, we had to carry our pickaxe, rope, and crampons.

"You can still change your mind," he said. "But when we get to the mountains, it will be too late."

I felt the weight on my back; it was heavier than I had thought, but the mountains were beckoning. I could do this.

The first days were amazing. The hike was incredibly tough, especially at large crevasses and steep climbing sites. I was struggling to keep up with the group. But a tall thirty-year-old had made it his mission to help me through those moments. At night, we all brotherly slept side-by-side on little mattresses and washed ourselves at the water pump outside. After a few days, the guide became more lenient toward me; I had lived up to my promise, which was a bigger relief than I wanted to admit.

On the fifth day, we crossed a long snowfield, and the sun mercilessly beat down on us. I had bought a special expensive sun cream for these kinds of situations, and I applied it thoroughly. But after a few hours of hiking, I started to feel sick. The guide urged me to drink more water. I plodded dizzily behind the group. When we reached the next cabin, my illness got worse, and I developed a fever. Sunstroke, was the guide's conclusion. I didn't believe it, because I had been wearing my hat the whole time.

The following day, I woke up with a strangely swollen face. Of course, the sun cream! I had suffered allergic reactions before: to certain types of food, to makeup. And my fever was gone. If it wasn't a sunstroke, I could continue, according to the guide. But I was hesitant. The whole day hiking in the sun with infected skin? I decided to drop out and told the guide I could go back by myself. The tall thirty-year-old wasn't too excited about that idea, but I didn't want him to break off his trip, and he couldn't persuade me to stay another day. With tears in my eyes, I said my goodbyes.

The climb down wasn't easy. I became dizzy and feverish again. When I finally made it back down, I took a taxi to the closest hospital. The first-aid doctor referred me to a dermatologist. A light sunstroke and an allergic reaction was the diagnosis. I got some powders and creams for my skin. The swelling would go down within a few hours, and I should stay out of the sun and take it easy, they advised me. After a few days, everything would be fine. An hour and a half later, I left the hospital entirely reassured.

I didn't feel like waiting for the group, to listen to their stories, or to wait for the bus back to the Netherlands. A train station was close to the hospital, and the station hall was nice and cool—a good place to think. I asked a nice lady at the ticket office if I could take a train to the Netherlands. She consulted books and train schedules, and I seemed to be in luck. In a few hours, an overnight train would go through Germany, with a change near the Dutch border in the early morning. The next day, I would be back in Haarlem.

continued

I will never forget that train ride. In the station hall, I felt the excitement of traveling alone—not on a bus with lots of other Dutchies to Austria. No, a train ride where I had to pay attention to where to get on and where to get off. Real traveling.

A few hours later, I was sharing a carriage with a German boy and girl who were traveling together. And far away from all the structures of life and our familiar surroundings, we had such fun, but we also aired our dirty linen. I did, at least, because I wanted to reveal something of myself. In the privacy of the carriage, encouraged by the darkness of the night and the dim lighting, I managed to open up.

"I don't visit my parents that often," I told them.

"Oh my," the girl replied. "I visit my parents at least once a week, otherwise my mum calls me on the phone."

The boy was playing with the little skull on his necklace. I couldn't see it that well in the dark, but I could hear it. "My mum bums me out sometimes. I can never fool her."

"Yeah, your mother's a witch." The girl laughed.

The boy stopped playing with his necklace. "If I'm honest, our conversations always let me look at my life from a different perspective."

"My parents and I just don't understand each other," I said. "They speak Dutch and I speak Chinese." I shrugged. "It is what it is."

"Mothers also understand you without words," claimed the girl. "We are created in their wombs. That's a connection that can withstand anything."

"Well, not with us."

The girl sat upright and stared outside into the dark night. "Okay, maybe not with you," she said.

The rhythmic sound of the rolling train wheels filled the carriage.

"You really don't feel that connection?" the boy asked.

His question sounded sincere and inquisitive. My cellar door was ajar, and I glanced over to the pile of dirty linen lying there on the floor. Did I have the courage to grab some of it? "It isn't that simple with us," I said hesitantly. I paused. "Emotions are not something we like to show at our house. Sometimes, I am scared that I am not even able to. That I am just like them."

The girl kindly touched my leg, which was lying next to her on the seat. "I think you are actually really sweet."

Tears welled up in my eyes. "You know, one time I was really angry with my mum, and I told her that I wondered if she actually loved me at all. She replied: 'But that one afternoon last winter, when it was snowing so hard outside, you were leaning against my knee, and I put my arm around you. Don't you remember that moment?'" Even in the dim light of the carriage, it hit me hard.

"Heavy," the boy said.

My heart was beating in my throat. "You know what I thought was heavy? That it only made me more angry. She was clearly trying her best, but I only felt the distance between us intensify. As if the fridge had been put on freeze."

The boy's head bobbed along with the movements of the train. "The answer just made you feel more powerless. That's why it made you feel like that."

"He knows that kind of stuff," the girl agreed. Loudly, she opened a pack of potato chips. "Care for a crisp?"

continued

I took one and put it in my mouth. Powerless. I could almost taste the word on my tongue, in my heart—it was salty. Powerless—I chewed it into tiny pieces between my teeth. I couldn't swallow it yet.

"And how about your dad? He was there too, right?" the boy asked.

I opened the cellar door a little more. "My dad is disappointed in me most of the time. About my choices, about my behavior. Sometimes I like to agitate him on purpose to make it worse. Recently, I told him that at the end of the month, I am always in the red at the bank. He hates that."

It's unbelievable how you can share so many intimate things with strangers. Or maybe that is exactly why, because they are strangers. Maybe it felt safer; they hadn't formed an opinion about me, and we would never see each other again after the trip. Aside from our dirty linen, we also talked about the purpose of life and about our dreams. I dreamed about traveling around the world. A different job. Leaving the security of the municipality. I had been working there for a few years now, and it was time to move on. To get out into the world. The journey on the train was a wake-up call.

Once home, I immediately quit my job. Of course, I had to pay my rent, so I started working for temp agencies. Life was beckoning, and with the temp jobs, I felt free to go wherever I wanted. The train ride had reconnected me with my source, and I could start living my first-choice life again for a while.

And yet, after a short period of time, I unknowingly slipped back into a second-choice life. Within the year I met a nice man, a teacher who played piano and wrote beautiful poetry. Shortly after that, I spent more time at his house than at mine, and we started living together. I disappeared again in a full-time job, his friends became my friends, and the longer we stayed together, the more I started walking his path—not that he forced me onto that; I just followed him.

The hikes through nature that I used to love so much became camping trips in France, where we visited castles. Salmon and tuna, my favorite food at parties, turned into spare ribs and hamburgers at the barbecue. Going out dancing became hanging out in bars with friends.

The sparse time I spent with my parents kept feeling laborious, and I stopped visiting my family entirely after a while. Aside from my sisters, I never heard from my parents or my brothers.

I was enjoying my life, but unknowingly, I was walking other people's paths again, not my own. Still, I hadn't learned to consider what I wanted from life. Traveling continued to be my clear passion, and I persuaded the teacher to go to Sri Lanka with me. A week before our trip, he broke his leg, so we didn't go. And after his leg was healed, we still didn't go.

After living together for nine years, I started to feel anxious, but I couldn't figure out why. We had spent some good years together, and I didn't understand why our relationship suddenly stopped flowing. We talked about getting married, but I didn't really want that. Fear of commitment, my friends concluded. I wondered if that was the case.

The teacher, who had always been sure of his path, had now turned into a searcher as well. In those days, there was a surplus

continued

of teachers, and he feared for his job every new school year. He could only stay as a teacher for the primary school although he enjoyed working with older kids. After a few years of hard work with little children, he had had enough and wanted to quit teaching. Working in a bar seemed good to him. He had gained some experience in the cafeteria at the local softball club, and the hospitality industry, working with people, really spoke to him.

He searched every newspaper for hospitality industry jobs, and I helped him. In those days, the jobs in that field were scarce, and our attention was caught by an advert about starting your own business in the industry. The best place to do this was Germany, according to the ad. His heart unlocked; he desperately wanted to have his own bar. But Germany didn't strike him as an ideal place. My adventurous spirit, however, saw the upside of it. The hospitality industry wasn't really my thing, but starting over abroad spoke to me immensely. We inspired each other with our plans. Because of my enthusiasm, he finally wanted to move to Germany, and because of his, I wanted to work in his bar. That's how we combined his dream with mine and ended up in Cologne. There, we became the owners of a cafeteria.

Two compromises. Two times a second-choice life. Of course, the venture didn't work out. I was extremely unhappy in the business. We had to deal with the hospitality mafia (a criminal group that guarantees your catering business's "safety" if you pay for it), and he missed his friends back home. After two months, we called it quits. In hindsight, it was interesting to see how we got stuck because we both started walking the other person's path.

After moving back to the Netherlands, the teacher worked as a waiter, and he flourished. I did not. He started drinking a lot at his new job, and I had a hard time dealing with that. Was this the life that I had been dreaming of?

The undefinable unrest continued to fester in me like fast-growing ivy. Still, I couldn't place it, and to point out a cause of all this unrest, I borrowed the fear-of-commitment theory from my friends. And to harness the unrest, we decided to get married. Wrong decision. At first, I felt like I was stuck in ivy that was fast growing up to my waist, but after getting married, I felt like it was swallowing me whole. But how could I explain that to him?

The first attempts came to naught and went something like this:

"If we continue like this, I am scared that it won't end well. I am unhappy."

"Why? Everything is going great. We're having fun, have a nice house, work could be better, yes, but that's part of life."

"That's not the point. I feel like something's missing."

"Oh? Like what?"

"I can't really explain it, but it feels like we're drifting apart."

"I haven't felt that at all. Can you give me an example?"

"It's not about examples. A feeling, it's a feeling."

"A feeling."

Silence.

"That is very vague, you see that, right? Just give me an example."

Silence.

"This is not the first time that you're stating this. I feel like I am entitled to an example now."

"But then the focus will be on that."

continued

"An example; otherwise, this doesn't make sense."

"Okay, fine." Silence. "I think you're drinking too much. You're different then. I don't like that."

"What is this all about? What do you mean different? I can handle my liquor very well." He crossed his arms. "Or is this about that one time? That whiskey just didn't sit well after that beer. How childish of you to bring that up."

"It's not about the drinking itself. It's about that you like to do that every weekend, and after work. I feel a sort of emptiness in that."

"First you accuse me of drinking too much, and then it suddenly isn't about the drinking. What do you want from me?"

Silence.

"What do you want from me?"

"I told you, I don't really know. If I knew, it wouldn't be so difficult." Silence. "But not a work-party-drinking life."

"You want me to quit drinking completely? To quietly sit at home with a Coke? God, you're such a nag. We're just having fun, that's it. A little booze helps to loosen up."

"You become aggressive. You're a mean drunk."

"That was just one time. You're making a big deal out of nothing. But if it will make you happier, I will pay more attention to it."

"It's not about making me happy. It's about your view of life."

"This vague bullshit again. But I know what I'll do, I won't drink whiskey as a nightcap anymore. I promise. Are you happy now?"

No, I wasn't happy, but I stopped talking about it. We got stuck in that example. He liked the drinking, the behavior, he enjoyed going out with his friends, and I wanted something else from life, from a relationship, something more fulfilling. That's what it was all about. I knew I sounded vague and he didn't deserve this, but I wasn't able to put my feelings into words at the time. The cellar door stood ajar, and I had no idea where to start.

I took a little break and went on a creative trip to France. We both thought it would do me good. But I wasn't even a block away from our house before I realized I would end the relationship. It was a light and calm feeling. Clear. Soothing.

I wanted to turn around and put all my cards on the table, but the voices in my head responded immediately. *You need this break. It will do you good.*

Who knows what insights you'll be getting there. And so they rattled on. Another issue was that I didn't look forward to breaking up. We hadn't even been married for three months. I thought of all the movies in which the bride or groom calls off the wedding the day before or at the altar. Why had I not done that? I agreed with the voices and talked myself into the idea of needing a break. Moreover, I had a friend who was joining me on the trip to France. I couldn't let her down, right?

I had great intentions, but the break didn't turn out as well as I had hoped. During the holiday I met a psychologist, who would later turn out to be relationship number three. He liked me, and I just went along with it. The newly wedded woman. What break? I had made my decision the moment I reached the end of the street, even before I met the psychologist.

When I returned, there was nothing left to do but tell my husband about wanting a divorce. The teacher didn't take it well. He became so angry that it scared me. I had left the tent in the back of my car; I quickly gathered some extra clothes from my wardrobe

continued

and drove off to the nearest campsite. He didn't come around. We only spoke through our lawyer. For the second time in my life, I left everything behind. And because I felt guilty, I also left the friend group. Meanwhile, I had turned thirty, and I had to start all over again for the second time.

The Empty Fairy Tale

I was living my life and did what was expected of me. It wasn't so bad (the *not-for-me comparison*). People appreciated my hard work on the job. The teacher and I had a good home and a lot of friends. I explained to others why my life was so good, great even. But something was gnawing at my soul. It didn't stop. I couldn't describe it; I couldn't explain it. The fairy tale was empty.

A part of me wasn't living life to the fullest, and after the first good phase of a relationship, I kept losing the connection with my source. I tried to find it in partners, friends, work, my career, in collecting things. I projected my desires and expectations of life on my partner, job, or anything at hand. In such a state, the other person, your kids, or your career seem responsible for making our lives worthwhile. And, of course, they don't. We get angry, and we blame it on our circumstances. But the gnawing continues. We are the only ones who can solve it. There are no shortcuts.

I see this often in my current job: people who are stuck in a gilded cage. They earn good money for their work and have the security of a full-time job, but deep inside, they are extremely unhappy with their job.

The Empty Tragedy

If your circumstances are complex, such as when I no longer saw my parents, it is impossible to tell yourself and those around you a beautiful fairy tale. In an empty tragedy, the mechanism works differently. You can no longer tell yourself that everything is going quite well, that there is nothing to complain about, as is possible in the fairy tale; no, your mind has to come up with other arguments.

I knew it wasn't going well with my relationship, job, or family. I felt unhappy, but I kept telling myself that it would be better soon, that my unhappiness was only temporary. If this or that was solved, or if my partner promised to start behaving differently, or if my employer promised me a wonderful job, and so on—yes, life would be better then. I was seeking an external fix as much as I had when I used the fear of commitment theory and got married to stop the gnawing at my soul. The empty tragedy was that I had no north star of *my own* to follow. Because I wasn't drawing from *my own* source. And the outside world would not help me stop the gnawing.

In the empty tragedy, we have lost the connection with our own source. Here, too, the gnawing at our soul continues. In the empty tragedy, life might feel tougher, and maybe you'll get more support from the outside world when you try to make changes than in the case of the empty fairy tale, but essentially, there is no difference. Whether we find ourselves in the empty fairy tale or in the empty tragedy doesn't really matter. In both cases, we make do with a second-choice life, and only we can set ourselves free. To do this, it is necessary to face yourself and accept the consequences of the decisions that have gotten you here. We learn to see clearly, without the voices in our heads, by reconnecting with our sources.

Have there been moments when you felt an inexplicable emptiness, a restless gnawing at the soul without knowing why?

NEVER-ENDING-EXHAUSTION

Never-ending-exhaustion is defined by living from weekend to weekend, from holiday to holiday. Being lived by your diary, your appointments. Finding it challenging to say no. Experiencing vague symptoms and attempting to slow down, only to realize that it intensifies the exhaustion rather than alleviates it. And the *never-ending-exhaustion* comes a-knocking. That is how I lived in those times.

There were moments when fatigue could be clearly attributed to specific causes, such as long workdays or staying out late and having to wake up early the next day. However, in the year leading up to my journey as an entrepreneur, I found myself enveloped in a pervasive weariness, unable to pinpoint its cause.

The days passed without feeling like I was truly alive—going to work in the morning, lying exhausted on the couch in the evening, repeat. If I had an appointment in the evening after a day of work, I already felt overwhelmed. On Wednesdays, I was always relieved that half of the workweek was over. On Friday, I thought: thank God it's almost the weekend. But on the weekend, there were social commitments, grocery shopping for the week, vacuuming, cleaning the bathroom, doing the laundry, seeing friends, and doing other "fun" stuff. Sunday evenings, I would again lie exhausted on the couch. The next day was Monday again.

In those days, I experienced that you can get really tired from doing the bare minimum and get lots of energy from working hard.

THE CLIPPED ROSE

Working and living in a tent wasn't easy, but luckily, I got to move into a furnished flat after a few weeks. The teacher had put my stuff on the side of the road, and when he wasn't home, I went to collect it.

Foolishly, I had given my phone number to the psychologist I had met in France (cell phones didn't exist back then). I called him to say that he should throw away that number, but I was too late. He had already spoken to the teacher. I wasn't planning to, but we decided to meet up. And that is how I ended up in a new relationship.

The psychologist lived in a new residential area in Alkmaar, and after four months, I moved in with him into his comfortable, well-insulated house with a sparmannia plant. The delicate leaves made me feel welcome. When I was struggling, I gently stroked the soft, hairy leaves with my finger.

The plant was resilient and robust, yet I yearned for Haarlem, for my old friends, and for the antiquated houses I once called home. Due to the ceaseless traffic congestion, I resigned from my job and secured one nearby, severing all ties with my former life. I embarked on a fresh start again.

The first year of the relationship with the psychologist felt strained. I almost broke it off during a trip to the Isle of Wight.

continued

I had fallen for his keen mind. As a psychologist, he could analyze people and events to the bone, put that analysis beautifully into words, and come to solid conclusions. Fascinating. But that keen mind also had a downside. He tended to be a know-it-all and thought he knew what I was thinking and feeling. Things went wrong when he started lecturing me during dinner at a restaurant.

It was a fancy, well-regarded restaurant because he had already planned in advance the best places to eat. In that fancy restaurant, I couldn't finish my entrée. I left two bites on my plate, and he wanted me to finish it.

I was too old for that kind of fuss, and I started to become mulish. He restrained himself and tried a different tactic. Of course, I shouldn't eat too much, but it was disrespectful to the chef. The chef had put all his effort into this dish, into the ingredients he had carefully assembled. And it was just two small bites.

We had a low-class fight in that upper-class restaurant and went back to the hotel. There, we stared out the window in silence at the sea that we couldn't see in the dark. Ultimately, we went to bed. The next day, I decided to give our relationship another chance. The two-bites fight seemed a bit ridiculous in the early morning light, although I kept pondering on the cause.

Back home, I remained a bit brusque—not because I wanted to end the relationship but because I also didn't want to put more effort into it. I felt tired and confused. We blamed the house. The psychologist also disliked the new residential area in Alkmaar, and we moved to the green and old village Bergen, his favorite place. With my new job and the move, I had enough going on to restrain the unrest. But something kept gnawing under the surface. That changed when we moved from the north of the Netherlands to the south (Zeeland) a year later.

The psychologist had been born and raised in that region. During a family visit, I expressed my desire to reside along the boulevard in Vlissingen. He promptly embraced the idea, and within a few months, we made the move to Middelburg.

He started a psychology practice from home, and I found a part-time job at a housing corporation, a sector I had enjoyed working in before when I was still living in Haarlem. A new adventure. New surroundings. The first few years there really put me into a flow.

Along with my part-time job at the housing corporation, I went back to night school. During my relationship with the teacher, I had received my degree in rental and resident business, and in Zeeland, I started studying commercial economy after work.

At first, I enjoyed working at the housing corporation very much. The job was varied; there was always something going on. I had nice colleagues, and my studies were challenging. I had balance. But after graduation, that challenge was gone, and so was the balance. I felt tired. At work, I was bored to death, and my colleagues suddenly became very conservative in my eyes. Every day felt the same. The fatigue worsened, and I thought I had caught some kind of illness every other week. I was stuck. I would have liked to do something else, but what? I felt so miserable at one point that I quit my job. I had to because all my zest for life was seeping out of me.

Financially, we could hold up for a few months without my salary. So when I sat at home, the question "Now what?" became louder and louder. I searched in every newspaper for a job; I

continued

was overqualified or underqualified for most of them. I applied everywhere but had no success finding a job within a reasonable distance of Zeeland. Now what? Now what? Now what?

The answer came to me when I was trimming the roses in our garden. I can remember it still. I thought of all the jobs I had experienced. Working for money was not enough for me. I wanted a job that also contributed to society. I started daydreaming and realized that companies and organizations occupy a fundamental place in society—and while daydreaming, I accidentally cut off a beautiful blossoming rose. Ouch! I was rudely awakened from my daydream and knew what I wanted to do. I hadn't gotten my degree for nothing; I could finally start doing something with it. That same day, I went to the Chamber of Commerce to enlist. I became an entrepreneur and started helping companies with strategic, organizational, and business issues.

It was incredibly exciting. My job search had cost me a lot of time, and my savings were almost gone. I wrote a business plan for my newly formed company and visited banks to request a loan. Two out of three said no, but the last one wanted to help me, so we were safe for a while.

The funny part was that one of the banks that didn't want to give me a loan mentioned my name to a company. That's how I got my first project. I also visited my former employer and the parties I had worked with at the housing corporation. Soon, I got more projects. It turned out I was very good at my job, and in my new role I started to grow and develop. It felt wonderful to be an entrepreneur. It felt amazing to help companies and employees make an impact. My diary was fully booked; I worked over forty hours a week. I started studying at Erasmus University. On the weekends, I was looking forward to seeing my friends again. Housework I did in between. If I felt like going to the beach on a workday, I let myself do exactly that. I felt alive and not at all tired anymore.

It felt almost inconceivable that only a month earlier I'd had to drag myself from weekend to weekend. Everything was tiring, and I had struggled with vague symptoms. I barely had the energy to vacuum and do the laundry. It felt like my part-time job had become a mountain I couldn't climb anymore. I was always tired during that time, but all those symptoms had now magically disappeared.

Looking back on those days, I have learned a lot. How easily I blamed the house in Alkmaar and the job in Zeeland. I felt extremely stressed in my part-time job. In hindsight, I see that I should have taken measures sooner.

Never-ending-exhaustion is a clear sign. I felt uninspired and tired, with symptoms that confounded me. Again, I unknowingly had fallen into a second-choice life.

If there was one period in your life that you wish you could just forget, which would it be?

SACRIFICE WITHOUT A STATUE

To me, sacrifice is one of the most destructive signs of a second-choice life. When we sacrifice, we think we're doing the right thing, but no one asks us to harm ourselves. By sacrificing, we feel obliged to do something for someone else. However, others want us still to be happy and do well. No one asks you to become overly tired or sick in caring for another or to stay in a sickening job to provide security for the family. They simply ask you for help, or the situation demands it, and others don't think about what that means for you. That part is yours to guard.

THE PSYCHOLOGIST AND ME

I was thirty-six years old, and suddenly, my hormones turned on. I really, really, really wanted to become a mother. So the psychologist and I married and began trying for a child.

Much happened during that period of wanting kids and being pregnant. The psychologist had started a partnership with a colleague psychologist, and the practice at home remained empty. At the same time, a detached house came on the market in a village only twenty minutes away from Middelburg, with a large garden. The asking price was the same as our property's sale price, and we called the real estate agent for a viewing.

The viewing started in the garden. It was the beginning of summer, the flowers were in full bloom, and an adventurous path ran between the trees behind the pond. The frogs were croaking, and the fig trees were beginning to bear fruit. It seemed like we had landed in paradise. Then we got a tour of the house. From paradise, we fell back to earth, and not even in a nice spot. Inside, the house had a brown, light diarrhea-beige color. Moreover, I felt a hostile you-are-not-welcome-here energy. The psychologist didn't feel that. He said it was probably the hormones from the pregnancy. It was just a matter of cleaning and painting. He was sure of it.

The real estate agent put pressure on us. If we wanted to have a shot, we had to put in an offer that same day because many people were interested. The psychologist thought it was a great opportunity; I loved the garden and let go of my hesitations about the house. And so, two months later, we moved into a house on a 1,500-square-meter (a little over two acres) property.

~~~~

In retrospect, we had a good laugh about our naivety. We bought a saw to trim the trees along the driveway and a riding lawn mower because the grass grew like crazy. The pond had a leak, so it had to be plugged up regularly. We struggled with a mole infestation. Every morning, we counted at least ten more molehills. When my belly started to become too big, I gave up weeding. When I reached the end of the row, I had to start all over again, and usually, it was too late anyway to keep the plot tidy.

Our plot was adjacent to a fruit tree company. With astonishment, I watched the clouds of poison that were sprayed onto the trees and then drifted onto our property when the wind turned in our direction. We were often startled by gunshots. In our neighborhood, there was plenty of hunting for pheasants and partridges. Men in high green boots and long dark coats scoured the plots in a fixed pattern. Those creatures didn't stand a chance. Country living also meant a lot of driving, whether going to work, shopping,

continued

or visiting friends. The figs grew but didn't ripen. Cleaning and painting the house only partially helped against that unwelcoming energy. The house barely tolerated us.

Ultimately, it meant that our paradise turned out to be more of a second job with poor employment conditions and surly accommodations. Funny enough, the psychologist seemed to struggle more with that than I did. And when I was at the hospital with preeclampsia, we bought a house that still had to be built in Middelburg.

~~~

I gave birth to a beautiful and healthy son at the hospital. A new energy awakened inside of me. I was going to care for and protect this tiny creature. I was bursting with an incomprehensible unconditional love that was almost overwhelming. Unconditional: before giving birth, I had known the meaning of the word, but only now I understood what it truly meant. Unconditional. Soft as the leaves of a sparmannia and strong as the sansevierias.

Meanwhile, selling our paradise didn't turn out to be easy. Many people had been interested when we bought it, but now we had to lower our price. With that lower price, we sold the house, and awaiting the completion of the new house in Middelburg, the three of us moved into a holiday home (a pay-by-the-week hotel) along the boulevard of Vlissingen. It was a fantastic place with a view of the Westerschelde, where large cargo ships sail insanely close to the shore. When the new house was finished six months later, I almost felt sorry that I had to move again.

The new house was adjacent to a courtyard, had a deck with a view over the water, and more families with young children were living there—a safe and comfortable place for a child. We started off well, but soon the psychologist fell ill. He became lethargic and had no energy. He wasn't able to work anymore. A few years earlier, he had become a heart patient because of a total blockage in which the AV node no longer transmits stimuli to the heart chambers, and for which he now had a pacemaker. We were wondering if the whole situation could have been caused by his new heart medication. The cardiologist thought this unlikely, but after several examinations, the new medication indeed turned out to be the culprit.

During the examinations, the disability insurance provided us with income, but with a new medication, the psychologist could return to work, according to the insurance. Physically, that was true, but mentally he wasn't able to. He had been worrying a lot during the weeks of the examinations. His father had passed away just before he was born, and he didn't want our son to grow up without a father too. The disability insurance didn't care and stuck to the decision that he could go back to work again.

The insurance money was no fortune, but when it was halted, we lost his whole income while the costs from his practice continued. After three months, that started to become a problem. Combined with the disappointing revenue from the paradise and the decorating of the new house, we had used up almost all our reserves.

After giving birth to my son, I had been working four days a week, but because of our financial situation, I felt obligated to start working five days a week again. It was hard, as I had grown attached to my special "mum-day," but we had no choice.

A year passed. The psychologist didn't make any attempt to start working again, his world became smaller, and he started

continued

focusing more and more on our child and me. It made me feel restless; I wanted him to start working again so I could go back to working four days a week. The need for my mum-day, when I could spend some alone time with my son, grew steadily.

One day, the psychologist surprised me with the announcement that he didn't want to go back to the partnership with his colleague. During his absence, they had hired another colleague, and it didn't feel like his practice anymore. I could imagine that, and we started to make plans. He could start another practice by himself. But Middelburg and Zeeland suddenly felt cramped: the limited job possibilities, the boring new residential area, and the one-and-a-half-hour drive to the closest big cities like Rotterdam and Antwerp. We came up with the idea of moving to Amsterdam. The psychologist could sell his share in the practice and would start over again after the move. For me, as an entrepreneur, Amsterdam would offer more potential clients.

We put up a "for sale" sign and started looking for a place to live in Amsterdam. We thoroughly enjoyed the days when we were viewing rental properties in Amsterdam. It boosted our relationship. After spending a few days in Amsterdam, we found a ground-floor flat close to the famous Magere Brug ("Skinny Bridge"). The characteristic old building had high ceilings, gas heaters, one bedroom, and a loft in the living room for our son. We couldn't wait to move in, and I was looking forward to spending my mum-days in Amsterdam.

Of course, we had to get rid of lots of our stuff—we moved from a single-family home to a small flat on the ground floor—but we made space for a big, tall plant. We chose a ficus benjamina, my new quiet friend.

Life in Amsterdam was more expensive. We shopped for our groceries at the local bakery, butchery, and greengrocer, and sat on the terraces of Amsterdam while our son was playing on the playgrounds nearby. And I rented a room in a multifunctional office building at the Keizersgracht, because there was no space at home to work out my notes or business plans. Every month, I had to earn quite some money, and I hoped my husband would start working again soon. But nothing happened. He needed just a little bit more time, he said. My anger started to fester inside me, but I kept it locked behind my cellar door. I also understood how we had been through many changes in a row.

Meanwhile, my son turned four years old, and he started attending primary school. The Waldorf school was located in the southern part of Amsterdam, twenty minutes by bike. Another reason why the psychologist couldn't go back to work.

"Do you know how busy I am with running back and forth? And you want the household to run smoothly, don't you?"

"I would like to do that."

"You would be disappointed."

"I would like to see that for myself."

"I can't make money that easily like you can. Give me some more time."

I decided to give it another go.

We taught our son how to ride a bicycle. We started out on a small brick square close to home. It was a cozy square where a lot of parents with young children gathered, surrounded by benches and terraces to keep an eye on their kids. We took the training wheels off, and soon the playground became too small for our

continued

son. With the bike on the back of our Greenwheels (a car-sharing system), we drove to the Amstelpark, where there was more space. My son loved the park, but around that time, he regularly started saying: "Mum, it's always so crowded here."

Even though we loved Amsterdam, we didn't have to think twice. We both put our child first, so that meant leaving the city. I focused on Haarlem, Bloemendaal, and Santpoort. The psychologist focused on Bergen. It became Bergen. A detached house, adjacent to the woods, was for rent. The spot was beautiful, but the house was one and a half times as expensive as our current ground-floor flat.

"I will go back to work in Bergen," the psychologist said.

And even though I knew better, I agreed with the plan.

~~~~~

Our last month in Amsterdam commenced, and I was cycling from my office on the Keizersgracht home across the Amstelveld square. And on that square—where I had played a lot of soccer, where we had taught our son to ride a bike, and where we had enjoyed so many coffees and teas while he was playing—exactly on that square, I was overcome by a gloomy feeling. Our relationship wouldn't make it, not even in Bergen. A vision formed. I was floating over the square, saw myself cycling, saw a woman stifled in her relationship who could not be herself, who felt pushed to keep earning money, and who failed to connect with her husband.

Screaming children playing tag disrupted my vision while the parents on the benches kept an eye on them. I got off my bike. We had a child together. Divorce was not an option. A ball rolled in front of my wheel, and a boy the same age as my son ran after it. *Stop it*, I said to myself. Don't talk yourself into things. It will work in Bergen. Amsterdam is just very crowded for all of us. I put my foot back on the pedal and cycled through the Utrechtsestraat, and when I reached the Kerkstraat, the vision faded.

Absent-minded, I arrived home. I wanted to start the conversation, but I didn't know how. My dirty linen syndrome now and then still blocked my ability to express myself. The psychologist was verbally much more skilled than I was, and what was I to do with all those vague visions? Later that evening, I made an awkward attempt.

"Is there a practice in Bergen or Alkmaar that you could join?" I started off the conversation.

"Let's move first; when we live there, I can start looking," he answered.

I understood that, but his answer didn't reassure me. The vision I had had on the square started forming again. "I am not very happy with the situation," I said.

"What do you mean? You're not unhappy, right?"

"No, unhappy is too strong a word." I always tended to be optimistic and to see the upside of something. I loved my child. He was always cheerful, exploring, curious. With him and because of him, I saw the world from a new perspective. The ficus benjamina was flourishing, and a walk in the park boosted my energy. In those moments, I thought of nothing except that the world was beautiful. The psychologist had a good and interesting side. He could cycle to the other side of the city to buy that special olive oil that gave the dish just that extra bite that it needed.

continued

In conversations, he was witty, smart and, with his psychologist brain, he could pinpoint exactly how something had come to be. No, I couldn't say I was unhappy; it was an unidentifiable feeling that I couldn't explain.

"From the house in Bergen, you'll walk straight into the woods," the psychologist said. "You'll love that."

We opened up a bottle of wine, and I convinced myself that Bergen would do us good.

~~~

We'd already lived in Bergen before, but it still felt like a different environment. There were now three of us, and we met new people at our son's school. Our son loved living near the woods and quickly made new friends at school. For me, Bergen meant a longer drive to work and my days were long, but I had more time for myself, too. Whenever I could, I took a stroll through the woods and the dunes just to be outside, even if only for half an hour.

The psychologist brought our son to school and picked him up in the afternoon, so it took awhile before I heard about everything that was happening around him. Unknowingly, a new reality developed. Proudly, the psychologist told every parent at school how we had divided the roles in the household. Suddenly, we were progressive. He was the stay-at-home dad, and I was the breadwinner. I let it slide.

How could I tell people who I had only known for a few months that the situation was caused by his illness, that he would go back to work again, and that I was looking forward to my mum-days? I didn't know how I could say that without making a fool out of him or publicly denouncing him. *Thou shalt not air one's dirty linen in public.* I still let myself be governed by the eleventh commandment.

I started the conversation at home. His response caught me off guard. The psychologist said that my view of the world was too romantic and that view was incorrect. Working suited me; I wouldn't be comfortable staying at home. I had a career, and I needed that. He had made all that possible. I was perplexed. He really seemed to believe it. At the same time, I was angry with myself. How had I let it come this far? I felt alone, rejected, estranged. My vision of being stifled in my relationship popped back up. I felt like I was stuck with a husband who always knew better, new people who thought we were the perfect couple, and my conviction that I couldn't divorce him because we had a child together. I started running off to the woods and dunes more often.

I don't know if the psychologist was truly happy during that time. Frequently, dinner wasn't ready when I got home. And we went out to eat more often. He started spending more money. We had more space, so the amount of stuff grew steadily. We had an oven, but we had to have a better one. Now we had two ovens. Grills, a special kind of frying pan, a paella pan, special tongs, a meat thermometer, poultry shears. There was no end to it. I said we had to start saving money. I couldn't keep this up. I felt like an ATM that was emptied out every day. I had to have a career to keep paying for everything.

I took on a project in Zeeland and stayed there a couple of nights during the week. That newly created space gave me the courage to say I couldn't go on like this. He didn't hear me. I wasn't

continued

convincing enough. Maybe I should have yelled and caused a scene, but those kinds of emotions were still locked away behind my cellar door.

The psychologist came up with a new idea. Back in the day, he had been a photographer at weddings and such, and he wanted to develop that skill further to turn it into his new job. I didn't know what to think of it, but because I had decided to make our relationship work for the sake of our son, I supported his decision. He went back to school, and it all started out well. He bought a professional camera, a slicer for passe-partouts, and books by famous photographers. This new outflow of money made me nervous, but I kept my spirits up. He shot a portrait of his brother that I thought was really special, and that fed my hope for a good outcome.

With his newly chosen path in life, my husband's status grew in the eyes of the school parents. A stay-at-home dad and psychologist who changed his life by choosing to pursue a career in photography. Astonished, I watched the process from afar. I had to admit, he could put his vision and the work of famous photographers beautifully into words. He always had interesting trivia ready and applied the ideas of these photographers to his own work. It made me enthusiastic too.

His search for fulfillment put something in motion in me. I saw how the psychologist chose himself and pursued his passion regardless of the consequences—for example, the costs that accompanied his new job and the fact that I had to work hard for that money. He just did it. He was the way he was. He hadn't asked me to give up my mum-day. I had done that myself. I could have caused a financial problem. Then it wouldn't have been my problem, but our problem.

I wondered when in the past few years was the last time I had chosen myself over other things. Being an entrepreneur and having a child were clear examples, but in the years after those decisions, I could not find a clear moment when I had done what I really wanted to do. My son was now six years old. Sure, I had loved seeing my child grow up, and living in Amsterdam had been a great adventure. But when it came to having something for myself, I had mostly worked, trying to make it work financially, to ignore the gnawing at my soul and to downplay it. And I was the only one responsible for that.

Within families, we take care of each other. Sometimes, we go along with the ideas of the other person. We temporarily walk the path of the other, sacrifice our own path, or postpone it. That other person unthinkingly takes up our space. Or: behind the scenes we work very hard and a colleague takes all the credit. Your coworkers don't seem to notice that this whole project would not have been launched without your contribution or would not have led to the same results. These are examples wherein sacrifice comes knocking on our door.

In my relationship with the psychologist, I was sacrificing my mum-day to maintain our lifestyle. This hurt me, and the stupidest thing was that I had made that decision completely voluntarily.

As I said before, to me, sacrifice is one of the most destructive signs of a second-choice life. Sacrifice is always destructive if it feels like a sacrifice. I had done so much to put my family first and swallow my needs. And for what? The psychologist hadn't asked for it. He just did what he did.

I had squandered my power, my truthfulness, my path through a misplaced feeling of indispensability, of being needed, of servitude to the assumed needs of another. In my role as sacrificer, I had expected a standing ovation, a tribute, maybe even a statue. After all, I was the one who had sacrificed everything. But everyone loves powerful, authentic people who stand up for their needs and passions. And no one ever notices the struggling, caring, and effacing wallflower.

With sacrifice, we end up in a second-choice life. And if we keep on doing that, we end up empty-handed, robbed, and burnt out.

What did you sacrifice?

Do you swallow your needs and do certain things because you think the other person needs that or otherwise gets into trouble?

When contemplating any sacrifice, ask yourself: when does it feel good for you, and when does it cost you too much?

Chapter 3

WHY YOU ARE LOSING YOURSELF

L ife seems to be designed to lose ourselves piece by piece from birth onward. As adults, we lose something we had as a child. We can't pinpoint it exactly, but it's the exception rather than the rule if we succeed to always avoid a second-choice life.

IT ALL STARTS IN OUR CHILDHOOD

As newborns, we arrive in a world that is unknown to us. Adults show up over our cradles. We have no idea who those giants are. They make sounds. We don't even know what sound is. We see vague images. Instinctively, we know that we have to stay on the giants' good side. They give us food and keep us warm. But they also do things we don't like, producing confusion.

We grow a little bit and smile at our parents. Crying, laughing. It works. But how it works, we don't know exactly. The giants teach us how to say mummy and daddy. Grandma, Grandpa. We learn the names of the mini giants, our brothers and sisters, the names of our pets.

As toddlers, we try to read and please the adults around us. Unconsciously. We like it when adults smile at us and tell us we've done something right. We so desperately want to do it right. We like the feeling of being seen. Herein, our mum and dad are the most important.

In our toddler phase, we develop the uncontrollable desire to investigate and uncover our surroundings. We are completely absorbed by it. Our siblings, our pets—we watch how they behave themselves. The other children in day care, kindergarten. Uninhibited, we let our source flow.

But the adults often intervene. They want to direct us, keep us, surprise us, and sometimes dominate us. For our own safety, to make us happier than they were, to let us experience things that they missed out on in their childhood. They stimulate us to keep delivering. According to grown-up ideas. According to grown-up rules that other adults taught them. There are also parents who can't deal with the responsibility of caring for their children due to depression, violence, alcoholism, abuse, and financial problems; the reasons are innumerable. We are too much to handle for them; we mirror their incompetence. In essence, we don't really do anything; we are just children, but our presence evokes powerful emotions.

Children pick up on both the powerful positive emotions and the negative ones. And even though the view of the road ahead can be quite different in an overprotective or unsafe environment, the outcome stays the same. We come up with a survival strategy. We try out strategies. We fine-tune our pleasing tactics, or we might completely shut down or think of other unhealthy patterns to cope with the situation.

Both strategies, pleasing or shutting down, are two sides of the same coin. When we choose to please, we violate our own desires, our own being; we step on the path of the other. When we choose to shut down, we build a dam. We hinder our source from flowing freely. We close ourselves off from other people and, in doing so, also from ourselves. Unfortunately, shutting down always causes problems for our own being, too. From behind the walls of our dams, we can barely show others who we are and what we stand for. By building a dam, we block both the outward and the inward flow. The source cannot flow freely.

SAUERKRAUT AND KNOWING WHAT YOU WANT

I was born in Sassenheim, in the west of the Netherlands. My father was in the flower-bulb business—half of my family, both on my mother's side as well as on my father's side, was in the business. Together with his three brothers, my dad worked the land that once had been his father's property. His parents had died when he was quite young.

We lived with my father's sister. After a while, the property became too small for the fast-growing families, and my parents wanted a house for ourselves. In the northern tip of Noord-Holland,

continued

there was plenty of space for a bulb business; my father took the leap and bought a piece of land and a small detached house just outside the village of Breezand. I was about four or five years old when we moved from Sassenheim to Breezand.

We had to work hard in the north. Without his brothers, my father had to do everything by himself. My mum tried to help where she could; she was a tough woman but physically frail, and she was often ill. We kids also worked in the bulb business. I mainly helped with selling daffodils, cutting tulips, and selling flower garlands to tourists during the season. I was too young for sorting, and I was too clumsy for peeling the bulbs.[1] To be honest, I was very clumsy in general.

I had trouble settling in Breezand and missed the Sassenheim surroundings. Looking back, it feels like a time when I both did exist and did not exist at the same time. There in the north, we had to rely on each other; the rest of my father's family wasn't there anymore. I felt lonely. My older sister was too old to play with, and my youngest sister was too young. My brothers only hung out with each other. We had no immediate neighbors, so I felt stuck between everything. The only playmates I had were the chickens and bunnies around the house.

Precisely during the first years in the north, the export prices of the bulbs were low. To earn some extra money, my father worked at a sauerkraut factory in winter. He never complained about it; we never aired our dirty linen within our family, but he found out that he could earn more money in a full-time job. The tension was palpable. As a child, I was very sensitive to moods and changes in the atmosphere.

Whether I hated the sauerkraut as a result of that tension or just because it's incredibly disgusting—I don't know. But because my dad worked in that damned factory, we ate a lot of sauerkraut in winter. And aside from "we don't air our dirty linen in public," we had another rule: You eat what is served. So I had no choice but to eat sauerkraut. I started hating Breezand and the tension at home more and more every day. Until one day, when I again was served a hot plate full of sauerkraut, I decided to run away. I pretended I had to go to the bathroom really badly. Secretly, I grabbed my coat, sneaked quietly out of the back door, and ran away as fast as I could. Onto the long straight road, along the cold, frozen gray fields, I ran and ran. Away from home, away from the tension. Away from the sauerkraut.

But before I could reach the village, I was caught. My father was trembling with anger. Back home, he put me over his knee and gave me a lengthy beating on my bare bottom. I suddenly felt the anger rise inside of me. I felt resistance against all those stupid rules. But instead of yelling or apologizing, I didn't say a word.

The obedience. The adapting. The eleventh commandment. I despised it. After that, I had to finish my whole plate. Cold, the sauerkraut tasted even worse. My mum watched how I ate the sauerkraut with tears in my eyes. She did nothing, said nothing, as always. Behind that plate of sauerkraut, something in me changed. My loneliness, the feeling that I was stuck, a relentless cold had been sown into my heart. I started to retreat into myself. Those were the days when the first seeds of keeping silent for the eleventh commandment were planted.

~~~

continued

Early in spring, my father taught me how to ride a bike. I had just turned five years old. The property surrounding us was waking up from its hibernation, shedding its blanket of hay off its back, and the first sprouts found their way up toward the sun. In a few weeks' time, the landscape would transform from light gray to soft green, then a colorful blanket of yellow daffodils, red tulips, and fragrant blue hyacinths. But when I was learning to ride a bike, my red bike was the only color visible that day. The neighbors closest to our house lived several kilometers away; the next neighbors were even farther. Their houses served as resting points on our circuit. My father told me to pedal as fast as I could and hold my handlebars straight while he held onto the bike and ran along with me. After running back and forth twice, my dad was out of breath and thought it was time I tried it by myself. Secretly, I was afraid, but I did it anyway. After several times falling off my bike and getting up again, I finally succeeded and proudly rang the bell attached to my handlebar.

After learning how to ride a bike, a whole new world opened up for me. I cycled farther away from home, discovering green patches with trees where I felt at home and fantasized about leaving Breezand. I was thrilled when my dad quit his bulb business after two and a half years of struggling. The export prices were still low, and my father had calculated that he could earn more as a quality inspector at the Royal Steelworks. Years later, I heard a song by Kinderen voor Kinderen (Children for Children). A girl sang that when she wanted something to happen really badly, it would happen. Now, I hadn't wished for the low export prices so my dad couldn't continue his business, but that was why we left Breezand. For a long time, I wondered if it was because of my wish that my father couldn't make it work in Breezand. I never meant that to happen. He had worked hard for it—maybe he felt like a failure, I didn't know—but because of the song, I felt a bit guilty about it.

From Breezand, we moved to IJmuiden, and there, my heart opened up. We moved into a house straight across from a park, close to the harbor. I could climb all the trees and build all the treehouses I wanted. With the canal, the dunes, and the beach all within reach, this was a great place to live. I made my first friends in IJmuiden. My parents were a bit more relaxed, which was great, but we didn't make a true connection. Still, it felt like an invisible wall kept us separated.

My mum sewed a wonderful lilac dress with black bows for my first communion, and my dad taught me how to play chess, but it wasn't enough. Back then, I didn't know that a dam stops the flow from both sides.

In our early childhood, all kinds of seeds have been planted. For one person, childhood is fertile soil for a sea of wildflowers; for the other, it's a neatly kept garden; and for yet another, it's a bush full of thorns.

What kind of seeds were planted in your childhood?

SCHOOL IS A SYSTEM

The time we spend at school shapes us. Together with the other children, we learn about the world from teachers and from each other. And if everything goes well, we get to know our personal interests and develop them with help from teachers. Unfortunately, many schools abide by rules, and the system decides what you learn. And in those systems, there's often a lack of time and room to consider the individual child, what motivates a child, what he or she loves to do, and where his or her talents lie. The system and the rules are paramount. Instead of encouragement, school systems unwillingly step on the souls of children, which causes a disruption in the connection with our source.

My son went to a Waldorf school. This sort of school stands for freedom—freedom from government involvement. The founder of the Waldorf school is Rudolf Steiner, and with its anthroposophical worldview, the Waldorf school pays a lot of attention to the development of the individual child. Every child can be who he or she is, leaving room for thinking, feeling, and conduct. The Waldorf school never used standardized tests set by the government because they thought those tests were too intense for young children. The child transferred from primary school to high school based on the teacher's advice.

That's how it had always been until my son started eighth grade. In that year, the district decided that the teacher's advice was no longer paramount for the transfer, but only a test result should decide which level was suitable for the child. So, even the Waldorf school was imposed with obligations. It felt like a bad dream. Suddenly, the children were no longer the focus, and the teachers were redundant. Only the test results seemed to matter. Even parents went along with the change. Low scores were debated. Parents demanded that their child should retake the test.

My son thought the test ridiculous and randomly checked the boxes. His teacher advised that he should be admitted at a higher level than the test result indicated. The Waldorf high school in our village, however, didn't provide classes for those who scored low on the test. I envisioned my son on his bike, with a giant backpack full of books, cycling to a massive public school in Alkmaar. But I also didn't want to put him through another test. With arguments like performance anxiety, divorced parents (more on this later), and no lower-level classes offered at the nearest Waldorf high school—the nearest that did was an hour-long drive away in Amsterdam—I convinced the school to help me out. He could try taking classes at a level a tad higher than was advised by his test result.

In my son's class, many students tested below standard; the children were not used to that system of questioning. They hadn't practiced it. Eleven- and twelve-year-old children who were once encouraged to be themselves were now judged for it.

The total development of the individual child—head, heart, hands—was not considered important in my day. Progress in math, reading, and writing was the only thing that mattered. The emotional side of a person was not discussed.

MY OWN SCHOOL REFLECTIONS

Around the corner of my house growing up was an elementary/middle school, but it was Protestant and we were not allowed to go there. We had to attend the Clara School, a strict Catholic school located farther away in the village. As a newbie, I went to the third

continued

grade of primary school. My teacher was a friendly older lady, Mrs. Heijdenrijk, who tried to make me feel comfortable. The teachers after her, however, were quite different.

In the fourth grade, the teacher hit you on your hand with a ruler if you didn't pay attention. In the fifth grade, I got detention for weeks because I didn't know the Lord's Prayer. At home, we always prayed before every meal, but I only mumbled along. At school, I had to stay in detention until I could recite the Lord's Prayer without stuttering. I was a good learner, but somehow, I couldn't recite it. It took me weeks until I finally got it.

After that, I started behaving more as I thought was expected of me, and so the time passed. But it's part of my nature that when the pressure builds up too high, my dam breaks. And that's what happened in sixth grade.

In the sixth grade, we were taught by the headmaster, Bart, a grayish man who had many rules. He liked to throw erasers and chalk at his students and viciously pinch their shoulders if they didn't know the answer to a question or briefly got distracted. We had to stay in detention often because, in his eyes, there was always something our class had done wrong. One day, we had to stay in detention again because one of our classmates had dropped a piece of paper on the floor. Outside, the sun was shining. I thought being detained was ridiculous, and when the bell rang, I wanted to leave. The world suddenly stood still when I walked through the rows of tables to the front of the classroom. My classmates seemed to be frozen; headmaster Bart stared at me like a statue. As if in a dream, I walked outside. I didn't have a choice; I had to break free.

The next morning, headmaster Bart didn't take me aside, but he informed the whole classroom that I had to apologize. If I didn't, our school trip would be canceled. My classmates stayed silent. During break time, outside in the schoolyard, everyone started cross-talking. The pressure was high. We were almost certain that he would cancel our trip. But I was struggling to apologize, as it wouldn't be sincere. I had no regrets for leaving from detention.

After school that day, I was the only one to stay in detention; the rest of the class was dismissed. I got a lecture and another warning that he would cancel the trip.

The lecture had left me speechless. A threatening sermon about hell and purgatory was nothing compared to this. Too much was at stake; a school trip was too big a deal. I apologized, even though I felt something break inside of me.

Middle/high school was the opposite of primary school. It was a public school with no church rules and chaotic management, and I went all out. My friend group was notorious for breaking the school rules. We were on good terms with only one teacher, but most teachers struggled with keeping us under control. After primary school, high school was a breath of fresh air for me. This was the same school where, with excuses, I could skip as many classes as I wanted so I could work at the fish packaging company.

Yet that is not what a child of that age needs. We got a new art teacher in high school who marched around the classroom like a modern-day Napoleon and liked sending many children out of the classroom. I held my posture because I loved drawing and I didn't want to risk being sent out. One day, I had drawn a picture of a spoon. I had sketched it in the style of Rembrandt and was quite happy with the result. I thought the drawing was really good.

continued

The art teacher disagreed. It wasn't neat enough. Something inside of me suddenly felt deeply sad. He didn't understand my creation. I felt rejection, not to be seen as an artist in the making. His reaction hit me disproportionately hard. In hindsight, that had nothing to do with the art teacher but with the constant feeling of rejection—while I was longing for encouragement, longing for help from the teachers and adults surrounding me.

Even with all the idiotic rules and punishments, in the end, I had a good time at school, mainly because of my friends. And also because of Mrs. Heijdenrijk, my third-grade teacher, who had provided me with a friendly and stable start in IJmuiden. But what I needed most—the encouragement from the adults around me, the room to be myself—I never got. The movement back to my source was cut off further in school. The walls of my dams unconsciously became higher.

School is a system, and systems can be supportive or can completely crush you. Which school experience has colored your view of the world?

A SECOND-CHOICE LIFE IS SAFE FOR THE PEOPLE AROUND US

I once saw an episode of *Help, My Husband Is a Handyman*. In that episode, the family of the self-appointed handyman had been living in an unfinished house for a while. His wife was at her wit's end. To the question of why she hadn't intervened earlier, she responded: "He only wants what's best for his family."

At home or at work, we laugh about situations that are actually too sad for words: "If Mary would see this, we would be in deep trouble." We behave differently when someone is or isn't around.

In every system, we fill a certain position: at home, in our family, at school, at work, at the soccer club. That position can be fine, or it can be a second-choice position, unconsciously developed in the passing of time. Nevertheless, we hold on to this position. Otherwise, the people around us might get angry or disappointed with us, or they may be forced to change their behavior when we say something closer to our hearts than the position requires of us.

When we consider the fact that it is part of our nature that we don't want to disappoint other people, especially our loved ones, that we prefer that our decisions and our behavior are approved by others, and that we don't like changes—it makes sense that we try to avoid stepping out of a second-choice life. The people around us usually don't want us to do so. When we lay out a different course of action and change our behavior, this has consequences for other people around us. Then, nothing can stay the same.

DEFYING THE ELEVENTH COMMANDMENT

After quitting the bulb business, my mum really wanted to have a job along with her regular household tasks. She was used to working, and we kids were growing up and needed less tending to. A vacancy for a hostess in the retirement home appealed to her.

continued

Enthusiastically, she told me about it. She already envisioned herself wearing a pretty dress, giving directions to people, helping them out, serving tea and coffee, and providing that little extra attention to make people feel comfortable. It had been awhile since I had seen that sparkle in my mother's eyes.

My father's response was protective. He didn't want her to work outside the home. He thought she had enough work keeping the house tidy. He reasoned that she had already worked hard in her childhood, that she deserved to rest after giving birth to five children and having the necessary surgeries on her womb and bladder, and that there was no need for extra income.

I thought my dad's response was patronizing and stood up for her. Being a hostess wasn't hard work, and a new environment could be inspiring. I said that my mum knew best whether she could handle it or not, and I talked her into taking the job. Clearly, I was young and foolish because I shifted all the attention toward me. My dad didn't want change. Now, his dinner was ready when he came home. And I didn't notice that my mum preferred to keep everyone happy instead of doing what she wanted. She defended herself by saying that it was mostly my idea for her to take another job. There I was, with two parents reproachfully staring at me.

"Do you want us to get a divorce?" she asked me later. I knew for certain that my dad would have accepted my mum having a job if she had pushed through, but I didn't want to risk airing our dirty linen anymore. In my dad's eyes, women working outside of the home were disgraceful to his own role in the household, and my mother obeyed him. Admitting that she longed to work at the retirement home would mean defying the eleventh commandment.

A second-choice life can be valuable in several ways for the people around us. At work, I was managing a young team manager who told me every day how well he was managing things in his team. Within the next three years, he wanted to be the regional manager and, after that, CEO. He made sure he was giving his team members a hard time; he ran a tight ship, but as soon as another team leader or customer made a comment about one of his team members, he stood up for the team member. When his people needed his help, he offered it. He worked obsessively hard and worked long hours.

When he'd just become a father, the situation at home intensified. He had a short fuse at work.

"Try to work four days a week," I advised him. "Enjoy your newborn child."

He responded slightly emotionally. "I have responsibilities at work."

"You also have responsibilities at home," I replied.

After a few conversations, the real reason emerged; to his family, it was very important to keep delivering and to hold a high position at work. His parents had invested a lot in him. He was the first in his family to attend university. "When you succeed in life, we succeed too," his father often said.

It is only human that people like it when we walk along with them on their path, even though it's not ours. They don't know that, as a result, we drift away from our own source. They don't see or feel it. They think it's the right thing to do.

Our environment usually isn't designed for changes. Keeping everything as it is is safe for the people around us: When you keep doing the same thing over and over again, they also can keep doing the same. When a couple in a group of friends decides to get a divorce, this affects the whole group, and it will never be as it was before. Even though change is the only constant in life, people don't like changing. We like routines.

Every morning, I wake up at the same time and eat the same breakfast. Before I go to work, I check my messages on Instagram, look at Facebook, and read the newspaper. Before going to bed, I read a few pages of a book.

Humans like set patterns. And people like it if their loved ones have set patterns too. Patterns provide stability. They make us feel like we have some control over our lives, that we are the captains of our ships, and that everything goes how we want it to go. We prefer to hold on to the familiar—even though that familiar thing makes us feel miserable—rather than surrendering to the unknown.

Our environment works in the same way. The moment we recognize that the people around us are happier and feel safer when we do what they expect us to do, rather than following our own flow, we can choose to let go. Or not. We can choose not to direct ourselves to our environment but to where the flow may bring us.

When we alter our course and change our behavior, it has consequences for the people around us. Nothing stays the same. A system changes when one person drops out or starts behaving differently from the rest of the group. Our environment usually doesn't like change.

What do you have to offer the people around you?

This chapter is called Why You Are Losing Yourself. I also could have chosen the title: Not Losing Yourself Would Be Weird.

My parents were born in 1931. They developed into young teenagers during World War II, a time when people kept silent for their own safety. No wonder they upheld the eleventh commandment so strictly. Unconsciously, they applied it to our lives. They had no evil intentions, nothing like that. The eleventh commandment was valuable for their environment.

Our environment has a strong impact on us, and it takes a lot of effort to keep following our own path in our everyday lives. When we learn to recognize these influences, we can learn to navigate better so that our source, the current of our lives, keeps determining our journey.

Chapter 4

YOU CAN'T KEEP UP A SECOND-CHOICE LIFE

When we start recognizing the signs of a second-choice life and see that we are more or less controlled by the people around us from childhood onward, you would think it would be easy to get out of a second-choice life. But that's easier said than done. It's for good reason that the golden formula for Hollywood movies' success consists of five plans, of which four fail. A second-choice life is safe and familiar, and our environment is used to it.

So why don't we try to make the best of a second-choice life? The simple answer is: we can't because a second-choice life ultimately does not make us happy; it lacks fulfillment, and we cannot sustain it in the long run. Our source wants to flow. There is a driving life force behind it that ultimately lets nothing stop it.

OUR SOUL DOESN'T ACCEPT NO FOR AN ANSWER

In a second-choice life, we intuitively know that we can't go on like this. The stagnant water of the source starts reeking. I myself always feel as if my soul is fighting a battle for life or death. The events, life lessons, and circumstances start to become more intense. Life is confronting me with my own behavior. My soul doesn't accept no for an answer. I can't continue living a second-choice life. And when I do, I feel like my soul is dying, like I am dead before my heart stops beating.

In religion, the soul has several meanings. We can't point out the soul, measure, or weigh it, although researchers tried the latter in the previous century. Dying people were put on a precision scale, and immediately after their death, they weighed a little less than an ounce (21 grams) less.[1] Was that the soul that had left the body? Or was it just air? The study has been suspended and labeled as unscientific. Maybe for the best. Because even though we give all kinds of different meanings to the soul, we don't really know what it is. Is the soul a feeling, something that moves us, or our (spiritual) essential self? Putting the soul into words is already difficult, let alone that we can come up with scientific proof.

NO SOUL, NO MUM

After I realized I had sacrificed myself without the psychologist asking for it and felt powerless to change my behavior within our relationship, I saw no other way out than breaking up. At the same time, I realized that when I broke up with the psychologist, I had much to lose. Somewhere deep inside me, I was convinced that it was best for a child that two parents stayed together. Divorcing—the idea alone already made my stomach turn.

For the psychologist, divorcing while parenting a child together was also unthinkable. He sought solutions. Our sex life had been dormant for a while, and he proposed that we could also live together in different ways. I didn't know exactly what he meant by that, and I also really didn't want to know. Freedom and the idea of doing everything different this time were beckoning. I wanted a divorce. My need for freedom was serious now.

The next day, the psychologist proposed that we should go to couples therapy—he had already found a therapist. I was surprised that he wanted to do therapy as a psychologist, but I agreed. During the initial consultation, the therapist asked us what we wanted the outcome of the therapy to be.

"That we will stay married," my husband responded immediately.

"A divorce, unless the conversations lead to a different outcome," I said.

"That's not couples therapy," my husband said.

"I won't guarantee beforehand that we will stay together."

"Splitting up in a loving way and with respect for each other can also be a goal," the therapist said. Thank God my husband had picked the therapist himself.

We arranged three follow-up appointments. The first one was for me alone, the second for my husband, and the third for us together.

My solo consultation with the therapist was intense. He thought divorce would be a missed opportunity; he had done research

continued

about love, and he tried to convince me that love was a verb with ups and downs.

"When you can overcome a crisis in your relationship," he said, "you can win so much more, also for yourself." He had published all kinds of papers about this subject, and he gave lectures to other therapists. That was, of course, the reason why the psychologist had picked him.

"It's a divorce, unless therapy leads to a different outcome and not the other way around." I stuck to my position.

"But the approach of staying together can still lead to divorce, right?" The therapist barely understood the difference.

To me, however, it made all the difference. My soul was fighting a battle over life and death. With divorce at my side, I felt more powerful. You might be thinking: couldn't you figure out what you wanted from life within your relationship? Yes, I could have, but not in this case. I wasn't there yet. I wasn't even close. I had not learned enough about following my own path. I didn't even know what that path should look like. And I didn't want to be overwhelmed again. Leading with divorce was my way of sticking to my position.

I don't know how the conversation between my husband and the therapist went, but he interpreted leading with divorce as proof that I didn't want to cooperate in the couples therapy. And that's how it came to be that I attended the combined therapy session by myself.

Then, the breakup went fast. We told our son that we were getting a divorce. We agreed upon co-parenting. My husband moved to a new rental flat. I booked available holiday homes and started searching for a permanent home in Bergen. And just like in my other breakups, I left all my stuff behind and started over again from scratch. Everything I had fit in the trunk of my car.

Meanwhile, I was in my early forties and for the third time in my life, I had to start over.

I had to cope with a lot, not only from the therapist and my husband but also from the people around us. And yet, I still took the leap. Almost nobody understood that my soul was slowly dying unless I broke out of this relationship. Within this relationship, I wasn't able—we weren't able—to turn the tide.

~~~

And no soul, no mum.

I suddenly realized that. Did I want to be a mother who lived as a zombie and who avoided living life to its fullest just to avoid stirring up the pot? So, even though it was the most difficult step I ever had to take in my life, I did it anyway. My soul didn't accept no for an answer.

It can be frustrating when no one can see that our soul is slowly dying in a second-choice life. We are the only ones that can feel it. And even then, we are not really sure of what we feel. The soul is an elusive thing. It's inexplicable; you can't point it out. But that doesn't make it less real.

Do you avoid specific conflicts in your work or in your relationship? Do you repeatedly encounter the same issues? With your kids? In your relationship? Does the subdued unrest never leave, even though you try your best to ignore it? Know that the soul doesn't accept no for an answer.

Might there be something that life is trying to tell you?

LIFE TALKS BACK!

In the long run, a second-choice life will harm us. Unhealthy patterns settle in, and when we don't try to escape them, we might suffocate. We experience difficult times at work, in our relationships, we get ill, we feel burned out, stressed, depressed, start drinking too much. Things have to change, whether we want to or not.

Water always finds its way to the lowest point. When a stream is blocked, the water will push as long as it needs to until it finds a weak spot in the dam or in the levee; it will find another route or the water will break through the barrier with all its force. Just like water, our source will find its way out. The source keeps pushing and finds our weakest spots until the moment our mental or physical problems become too big. Then, the source breaks through our unhealthy patterns and choices with power so that we dare to take the steps necessary to deal with what is essential at that moment.

My relationships always started out promising, and yet the outcome was always the same. During the first phase, I was always connected to my source, but later on, I unknowingly slipped back into a second-choice life. I didn't communicate enough, didn't share my true thoughts and feelings openly. I didn't air my dirty linen in public. More and more, I fell silent by keeping everything to myself. Not because I wanted it. It just went like that. It was my dirty linen pattern.

With those dirty linen rocks in my source, I closed myself off. Not only from the other person but also from myself. I was blocking the source. And when the source stops flowing, life talks back.

The lessons become tougher and tougher. You find yourself back at the same crossroads. It happens to you again.

REPETITION OF MOVES

I started seeing a pattern in my relationships. It started with the gnawing at my soul, the feeling of an indefinable emptiness, not knowing what was going on, what to look for, and where to look for it. I didn't know what I needed, and I wasn't able to communicate those feelings to my partner. Slowly, I started losing myself, and suddenly, the relationship felt stifling. The only way out was breaking out of that relationship, no matter the consequences.

Suddenly, I figured out a pattern. It was hard to acknowledge, but I discovered a repetition of moves. And I had caused them myself; I was the only one to blame for my own behavior. If I didn't learn to stand up for myself, if I didn't learn to talk about what I found important in life—even though I didn't have the words for it—if I didn't learn when to confront the other person, if I didn't start learning all that in a relationship, the outcome would always be the same.

Looking back, I saw that life started talking back to me more often. I moved in with the tall, quiet boy without asking myself if I wanted that. The breakup was painful for the quiet boy, and how it all worked out was not something I was proud of. Life was whispering back at me.

It became worse with the teacher. After nine years of living together, I reinforced my dams by marrying him, which resulted in

continued

such high water pressure that the dams broke within three months. Life was talking back at me loud and clear. I felt ashamed about that action for a long time, and I never told new acquaintances that I got divorced after only three months of marriage.

I married the psychologist and we had a child together. I gave up my mum-day. I gave up my own space. Divorcing had long not been an option because of my son, and yet, in the end, I had no choice but to get a divorce. Otherwise, I couldn't be the mother I wanted to be. Life didn't just talk back at me, it was screaming in my face.

The moment we stop living our lives to the fullest, the gnawing at our soul commences. When we keep throwing all our dirty linen, as well as our wishes and dreams, in our cellars, they will get smelly and moldy. When we keep ignoring the signs, downplay them, shout over them, and park them away, life will start talking back to us louder and louder in a way that can vary for everyone.

A person might develop mental problems or physical illnesses. We end up in unhealthy patterns. "I attract the wrong men or women," people say. "I always encounter problems at work": an obnoxious manager, work pressure, an annoying colleague. "I am always the unlucky one." Of course, circumstances can lead to unhealthy situations, too. But there are also circumstances for which we open the door ourselves by stifling our potential, adapting too much, suffering in silence, or causing fights. Deep down, we often sabotage ourselves, hide ourselves behind the walls of our fortresses, or strengthen our dams. We prevent our source from flowing.

In my work, I see many young people who are coping with burnout. They are living the lives of others instead of their own. Depression runs in my family—the feeling of a void, emptiness, pressure and heaviness, lethargy, seeing no way out. A second-choice life can activate that disposition.

My subdued tension expressed itself mostly in fatigue. Especially in my twenties, I caught one illness after another—slow bowel movement, intestinal parasites, glandular fever.

Subdued stress causes problems in our biological system. Sometimes, we give it an extra push by eating too much or not enough, by drinking too much alcohol, or by working out too fanatically. We blame everything and overlook the real cause. We often try to find the solution in food, exercise, underlying medical causes, getting enough sleep, moving, divorcing, and so on. Those actions can be effective, but when the symptoms are also caused by a second-choice life, the symptoms will always resurface. Like a hydra from Greek mythology, you cut off its head and three new ones appear.

Until that moment when *seen* becomes the echo of *unseen*, we realize: oh, that's why living a second-choice life is a problem!

When we keep ignoring the signs of a second-choice life, life starts talking back. In the beginning, it will only whisper—we might not hear it correctly. But over time, it will become louder until life doesn't just talk back, it screams in your face.

Which recurring pattern is screaming in your face?

THE WORLD IS INCOMPLETE WITHOUT YOUR UNIQUE CONTRIBUTION

Osho, an Indian mystic who mixes Eastern philosophies with Western therapeutic techniques, puts this concept beautifully into words. "You are not accidental. Existence needs you. Without you something will be missing in existence and nobody can replace it."[2]

Every person is unique, and everyone contributes to the whole. Through living a second-choice life, we leave our unique space open. We don't recognize our own role. It feels like something is missing. Our spot cannot be traded or filled in by someone else.

Hesitantly, we observe others. How are they coping? We look for help in the *not-for-me comparison*: she can do this better, that colleague is smarter, he is better off than I am, I am actually doing all right, should I be doing the same? But it doesn't matter; everyone is unique and everyone contributes to the whole.

Does the dandelion ask itself if the rose that's blossoming next to him is more beautiful or better than he is? No, the dandelion just does its best to grow—when needed, the flower even pushes itself up through the concrete. In early spring, it unfolds its yellow flowers. And with those flowers, it gives life to bees and butterflies. Not many other flowers bloom so early in the year and in such large numbers, and in doing so, they welcome the bees and butterflies back from hibernation by feeding them with nectar and pollen.

After the dandelion has the chance to let its yellow halo shine so beautifully, its leaves close, and the flower transforms into a white furball, into countless fluffy parachutes for the seeds, which, helped along by the wind or the blowing of a child, fly out for a new, unique existence.

By comparing ourselves to others, we disconnect ourselves further from our source. Like the dandelion, we all have something valuable to contribute. But we are not used to looking at our situation like that.

We find it easier to see the contributions and sources of celebrities. Vincent van Gogh tried everything to live according to his passion. After first trying out some other paths, he discovered painting. And he wanted to paint whenever he could. He didn't care that he had to live in a small room, that he was admitted to a mental asylum. It seemed he had no other choice; he had to paint. During his life, his works weren't worth much, although he inspired other artists around him. After his death, he entranced millions of people with his works and inspired countless more painters.

Art has the power to touch the soul. When something from the soul, the source, is created, it touches something deep inside—something universal. Art, music, dance, and poetry can touch us so deeply sometimes that we think only true artists can achieve this. Or people like Gandhi, Nelson Mandela, or Martin Luther King. But that couldn't be further from the truth. A chef who creates an amazing dish can achieve the same. A neighbor who picks a flower or brings us a bowl of warm soup when we are sick can achieve the same. We are touched continuously, and it resonates in our source. We are all artists in our own way.

CEO FOR THE FIRST TIME

When I started out as an entrepreneur, I mostly created business plans for organizations. I made one for a childcare organization that had to deal with staff shortages, waiting lists, pressure on liquid assets due to a slow response from the government, and the rapid growth of the organization. At the head was a young decisive CEO who wanted to steer the growth of the business in the right direction and advocated for sufficient and pedagogically sound childcare in the region. We got along well together and made plans.

The ink of the business plan was not yet dry when the CEO received some bad news. She was pregnant, and the pregnancy wasn't going well. She had to rest immediately; otherwise, the baby would be in danger.

"Now you'll have to lead the company until I come back," she said.

"Huh?" I had never been CEO before, especially not in an organization that was struggling. "I am not sure if I can do that."

"Of course, you can. People listen to you."

The latter was true—the managers to whom I had proposed the business plan had been skeptical at first, but now they were completely backing me. "Yeah, that might be true, but I am not like you."

"I already spoke to the board, and they agree with me. We won't find another on such short notice that is suitable for this position."

I caught myself comparing myself to the CEOs I had met. The dandelion doesn't ask himself if the rose is better—the lesson I had recently learned popped into my head. *Why do I keep doing that, comparing myself to others?* I wondered in annoyance. Just determine if you expect to be able to do it.

"Okay, I'll do it. But you will come back, won't you?" Even though it was scary, it was time to push myself up through the concrete, to be courageous, and to show my halo to the world.

"Good, it's settled then," she said with satisfaction. "Then I'll be going home now. If there's a problem, you know where to find me."

It turned out to be a tough period; the funding of the municipality arrived barely in time for the salary payments, we had an incident with a caregiver who threw a plate against the wall while having lunch with the children, and we worked hard to get the organization back on track. Strangely enough, my profile turned out to be a perfect fit. I turned out to be calm and clear, knew how to keep to the plan, and knew what I wanted. The business became more organized, and the municipality was cooperating. My unique contribution was welcomed during that time.

The CEO gave birth to a healthy baby, and after a few months of pregnancy leave, she came back to claim her spot. I was relieved about that. I wanted to return to my new, exciting entrepreneurial projects. It was also good for the organization. The CEO brought continuity and a strong pedagogic policy. That was her unique contribution to help the organization along.

The world is also waiting for you, for your unique contribution to the whole. Existence needs us, and we deserve to live with a strong connection to our source.

This principle is true for all sorts of lives—a simple life, a creative life, a successful business life, a busy social life, or a secluded life. What matters is that we take in our space and live to our full potential.

> *Existence needs you. You can't trade your unique space with another. Your space cannot be filled by another. Without you, something in existence would be missing that no one can replace.*
>
> *When did you inspire others by accepting your unique space?*

IT'S DIFFICULT TO ESTABLISH EQUAL RELATIONSHIPS BEHIND DAMS

Our biological system is created to cooperate. To be seen, to gain respect, and to gain trust are some basic needs. Traditionally, we used to live in tribes, and the mutual relationships are necessary for our happiness and well-being. It is, therefore, essential that we start living according to our source. In a second-choice life, we rarely enjoy relationships where we are fully open to one another because we have shielded off a part of our source. We have built dams, retreated in our fortresses, and closed the shutters when things were about to get interesting. Our reaction is then invented and no longer spontaneous. The source is not flowing. From behind the dams and the stagnant water, we try to make contact with the other, but how can we enter into an equal relationship when we have blocked ourselves?

Unfortunately, for establishing a real relationship with my father, I recognized the mechanism too late.

THE LAST TIME I SAW MY FATHER

In my childhood, I didn't have much contact with my father, except during our holidays in the mountains. Those were some amazing weeks. As much as he loved to analyze the moves of his chess computer, he also loved to arrange the hikes in the mountains during our holidays in Austria, Switzerland, and Northern Italy. The end goal of the hike was always a cabin.

During those hikes in the mountains, I always felt deeply connected to my father. We found each other in hiking, in the mighty mountains, in the reflecting lakes, and in the flowers in the meadows of the Alps. We loved listening to the whistling sounds of the groundhogs and the jinglejangle of the cow bells.

Hiking in that wild nature meant that we could connect without words.

We enjoyed ourselves alone, and we enjoyed ourselves together. Once we arrived at the cabin, we ate spaghetti or Wiener schnitzel, and I would drink a bottle of Orangina. We shared fun stories about our trip: the dangerous little pathways, the impressive scree we had climbed, the groundhogs we had spotted, and the spectacular mountain ridge. And on the map, we searched all the names of the mountain peaks around us.

But as soon as we got home, that special connection my father and I shared was gone. We started talking again through our walls, behind our self-built dams. Those dams were heightened

continued

when I moved in with the tall, quiet boy. During my father's rare visits, we talked about safe topics, mostly about stories featured in the newspaper.

This continued until the time I started seeing the teacher. The way my father and I had found to get along with each other suddenly didn't work anymore. There were uncomfortable silences. I felt something had happened, but I had no idea what it could be. My parents didn't mention it, and I didn't ask any questions. Our dirty linen still didn't air in public.

I decided not to visit my parents anymore to see what would happen. Nothing happened. We had no contact anymore. For about ten to twelve years, we didn't see each other until I moved close to their neighborhood in Alkmaar with the psychologist. I worked my courage up one day and rang the doorbell. My parents welcomed me happily, and our old way of connecting, talking about safe topics, worked again. We didn't say a word about the past ten to twelve years.

But not even a year later, something went wrong again in the relationship with my parents. The psychologist and I moved to Zeeland, and because of the distance, when my parents came to visit, they stayed over for the weekend. They hadn't been there for half an hour when my mum started talking about their upcoming fortieth-anniversary party. She was filled with joy about it and assumed I would come. Our renewed relationship was moving way too fast for me. We had just reconnected again, and now they were here for a whole weekend, followed by a big party? In response to whether I would come, I carefully said: "Probably not, but maybe, who knows."

"Of course you'll come."

"Don't count on it, we'll see."

"All our children have to be there."

I had kept in touch with my sisters but hadn't seen my brothers for ten to twelve years either. "I don't think so."

My mother didn't give in. "A good daughter doesn't do that to her parents and just shows up."

"Well, I won't."

My parents were disappointed; they had always taken good care of me, right?

I was also disappointed, and I reacted fiercely. Yes, they had provided me with food and shelter, but with love? Where were they when I had to go to the police station? Where were they when I was a teenager and someone close to me cornered me and touched my breasts? I hadn't even had time to process the incident with my boss from the fish packaging company.

My mother fell silent. My father thanked me that day for not making a big fuss when I was a kid. He thought it was a good thing that I never argued with anyone, that I retreated into myself. He thanked me again. He seriously meant it. It fit in his view of the world; it fit in his comfort zone. That day in Zeeland, the gap between us widened. That happens when you're both living in a second-choice life. It seems like you have no other choice.

When my father expressed his gratitude, it deeply hurt me, even though I couldn't fathom why. Now, years later, I occasionally ponder: what if I had made a significant fuss about it? I wish I hadn't accepted his thanks or withdrawn into myself. Perhaps then, we might have established a genuine connection, like the

continued

one we had when we ventured on hikes and I could converse with him. I longed to pose various questions. I wanted to inquire about his experience of leaving the bulb business to enter paid employment, why the eleventh commandment held such significance for him, and what it was like for him to lose his parents at such a tender age.

My father passed away the same year my son was born. After that day in Zeeland, I never saw him again.

I have noticed that my relationships deepened and improved when I started living according to my source. The relationships became closer, I was able to show more of myself, and that was an invitation for others to show more of themselves, too.

Besides deepened relationships with others, I also developed a better relationship with myself, which improved both my physical and mental health. I became more relaxed. Deep within, I found a calm anchor point, something that had always been there.

When we start living according to our source, we get the opportunity to build relationships from equal worth.

When we construct dams in our stream, we find ourselves in stagnant water. It becomes challenging to foster a full-fledged relationship when these dams impede the flow. We become isolated from others and, just as crucially, from our true selves.

In which situations are you now contemplating, "What if I had revealed my authentic self?"

Looking back, I am mostly surprised about the way I tricked myself. It started with the fishy incident in my childhood when I told myself that it was a good thing that I didn't tell my friends about what happened, but later in life, this pattern kept repeating itself. In times when I wasn't doing well, I told myself that my life wasn't that bad and that it would improve over time.

It wasn't until my early forties that I finally figured out the signs and the patterns of my second-choice life. And it was the plum tree in my garden that helped me understand how I started tricking myself.

After divorcing the psychologist and taking some detours via temporary homes, my son and I planted a plum tree in the garden of our new house. The first year, that tree bore beautiful fruit. But in the second and third years, it produced less and less. I didn't know why and started looking for explanations: Maybe it had rained too much or not enough the year after. There had been frost in early spring. I hadn't pruned the tree correctly, I should have thinned out the fruit, and so on. When it hadn't rained for a while, I gave the tree some extra water. I looked up in all kinds of books how to prune it. I wanted to wrap the tree cozily when the temperature dropped in March. I kept searching for explanations until the tree bore no fruit. I hoped it was skipping a year; the internet had said that that could sometimes happen with plum trees. The year after that, I really started worrying and found a tree surgeon.

"The tree is planted in poor soil," he said when he came over. "Some fertilizer will work wonders."

"Really?" I asked. "Is that all?"

"Yes."

"Okay." Why hadn't I thought of that myself?

"Don't worry, there are more people who just keep muddling on without really addressing the problem." He also told me that he had visited a large villa the week before. The plum tree stood there in the enormous garden, just a little too much in the shade. That was because the trees behind the plum tree had grown into tall, mature trees over the years. The once sunny spot of the plum tree had turned into a dark, shady spot. The owners had not noticed this.

~~~

Like the plum tree, I hadn't borne fruit in some periods of my life. And, of course, I also tried to find explanations during those periods. But I had searched for the obvious reasons like I had done with the plum tree. It is extra confusing that a second-choice life and a life in contact with your source can walk side by side. Sometimes, my working life was in connection to my source, while my personal relationship had ended up in a second-choice life, and vice versa. My first- and second-choice lives interchanged, unknowingly. And the warning signs I received, I tried to explain to my advantage. If I saw the signs at all, I ignored them, pushed them away, or labeled them as either impossible to address or something that everyone struggled with. I hadn't heard of a second-choice life yet.

How wonderful it would have been if I had recognized the signs of a second-choice life at that time. It would have saved me from many detours. But when I finally recognized the signs, I was ready for the preparatory work to live a more conscious life from my source.

Part II

LIVING A LIFE
FROM THE SOURCE

Chapter 5

ON THE THRESHOLD, THE PRELIMINARY WORK

Great! We're standing on the threshold to restore the connection with the source. Stepping out of a second-choice life can be compared to rafting on a river. We would like to be carried away by this source, but we keep asking ourselves if the water isn't too rough, too cold, or too deep. We can see ourselves going under, not knowing if we will be able to come back up again. Preliminary work can help to prepare us for our journey.

This chapter is all about that preliminary work. Just as we turn up the soil before we start sowing seeds, it is essential to do some preliminary work to restore the connection with our source. Will you come along and step over the threshold?

LOVE ME: PUTTING YOURSELF FIRST; THE REST WILL FOLLOW

Love me means putting yourself first, loving yourself no matter what you do or what you look like. It sounds easy, but it's incredibly difficult. Think of it as the procedure for putting the oxygen masks on when the air pressure in the plane drops. First, we have to take care of ourselves, help ourselves, before we help others or our children with the masks. In a second-choice life, we are used to adapting, hiding, or outvoicing ourselves, and it is hard and scary to try and change that. With *love me*, by putting ourselves first, we find ourselves on new terrain. We don't know exactly what to do. And we wonder how other people will respond.

I had developed a way to know what the other person needed. At least, that's what I thought. With my optimistic nature, I didn't think too much about whether what I got into was also serving me; I simply did what I thought needed to be done. And when it all got too much for me, I had to break free, become wayward for a while, and then silently adopt my old role again.

By taking *love me* seriously, we start restoring the connection to our source. These are the first steps.

SURROUNDED BY ORANGE TREES IN ANDALUSIA

After divorcing the psychologist, I was prepared to go to the ends of the earth to start following my own path. Finally, I was free to do whatever I wanted. I was ready, I was motivated, I was looking forward to it—but suddenly, I realized that aside from traveling, I had no clue what my true passions were or what I wanted to do with my life. It was a miraculous discovery that I hadn't counted on.

I started working on myself. My insights about the repeating patterns in my relationships were clear. The dirty linen syndrome reared its head repeatedly. I understood that a second-choice life not only isolated me from others but also from myself. And I understood that when I had completely lost myself, I also lost contact with the people closest to me and my friends. At least that insight was a good start.

Finding out what my passions were and getting to know myself was the next logical step. I booked a retreat in Andalusia.[1] *Reconnect with yourself and discover your strengths*, it said on the website. That was exactly what I needed. The former monastery, situated in the rolling hills and surrounded by orange orchards, made the site even more appealing.

The group consisted of eleven women and one man. According to Arthur and Jivan, our supervisors, this rarely happened, and normally, the groups would be more mixed, but I was fine with it. Falling in love was the last thing on my mind. I told myself that finding out what I wanted from life wouldn't be possible in a relationship. I had proven that to be true three times. Other people might be able to do so, but I wasn't there yet. Not by far. I hadn't learned enough about following my own path. If it wasn't even clear to me what that path should look like, a new relationship would prove to be a major impairment. Unconsciously, I recognized the subdued feeling of unease, of not being connected to my source. In those moments, I had to break free and follow my own path for a while.

continued

Still, consciously, I couldn't grasp my source yet. I could not yet distinguish between what was and what wasn't important to me.

Most of the participants shared a room with another person, but I had permitted myself the luxury of booking my own private room. It was a sparsely decorated room with sandstone walls and sturdy wooden frames, but more spacious than what I had expected from a room in a monastery. I was extremely happy having my own room because a group could be quite overwhelming for me.

We started the day by meditating, I got to know some chakra exercises and came closer to myself during silent hikes. I had no problem being quiet on my own. During my hikes through the woods or the dunes, I found it easy to be silent and to feel connected to everything around me. But it was a whole new experience to be silent in a group of people.

We started the first silent hike from the monastery. We hiked all the way up on a small path between the landscaped fields with orange trees. It felt uncomfortable to walk next to other people and not say anything. Secretly, I looked at the other participants. What were they thinking? Did they also feel as uncomfortable as I did? Even though I didn't talk, my head was everything but silent.

A small, sleepy village with houses of thick, irregularly shaped stones and small windows briefly interrupted my maelstrom of thoughts. I admired the cactus plants with profusely blooming red flowers in their gardens.

After the village, we turned into a rocky forest path. Longingly, I looked at the trees and undergrowth, but I couldn't seem to blend in with the surroundings this time. The group got in my way. In my head, all kinds of thoughts were swirling around about the other participants and about what this journey could bring me. Eager to feel the energy of the environment, I resolved to walk this trail again on my own if I had the chance.

After twenty minutes of climbing the forest path, Jivan halted. The group dissolved. Some looked for a rock or a tree trunk to sit on; others scrabbled between the trees and picked up sticks or a beautiful stone. Oh right, I remembered—after the hike, we would share what we had taken away from this hike—an impression, a thought, or an object that spoke to us. I leaned my back against a tree. I picked up a broken twig and waved it around.

I kept the twig when we continued our hike. I don't know if it was the twig or the length of the hike, but suddenly my head fell silent. I started to feel a connection to the people around me in silence, even though I barely knew them. It was fragile, but for a minute, I felt that I could be completely myself in a group of people with no thoughts, without wanting to meet any expectations.

When we arrived at our end goal—a café in another sleepy village—we exchanged experiences. I mumbled something about feeling some sort of connection with the group. But the fact that I could be completely myself in that connection, I kept for myself. That was something I had to investigate further. Being myself in a group of relatively new people was new to me. Maybe I had imagined it. I couldn't answer any questions about it—the experience was still too fresh.

During that week, we also did an energy exercise in which we had to connect with another participant. We had to read each other by tuning in to the higher self of the other and seeing what kind of information we would get from them.

continued

Sitting across from the other person, we held each other's hands. Our eyes were closed. First, we connected through the heart chakra, until we could feel the energy pass between us. After the connection was made, we could focus on the higher self of the other. You could receive information that might be important for the other: their passion, strengths, or a direction.

I don't know if the cosmos had a plan for me, but of course, I had to do the exercise with a woman who was looking for her knight in shining armor. She desperately wanted to fall in love and meet the love of her life. She had told us her life goal at the start of the retreat. During the exercise, I was uncomfortably surprised by the fact that she wasn't actually looking for her knight in shining armor but for her own space—a space that was meant for her, designed in a way she liked. I mustered up the courage to say that there was no knight in shining armor on the horizon but that her higher self wanted a place of her own. She teared up when I told her the message. After a brief silence, she thanked me and told me that she had also gotten that insight the past few days. She recognized that she had paused her whole life in search of her true love. She had postponed decisions about the interior of her house because she might not live there much longer. *Love me* comes before *love you*, I would say in that situation, but I didn't know that then.

She also had a message for me: *Sit on your favorite dune top at sunrise, and your passion will be revealed to you.* That's all she had picked up. I was annoyed. Aside from the fact that I hate getting up early, now I also had to wait until I got back home. And I wanted to know it now, NOW. Yet, when I arrived back home I didn't immediately go and sit on my favorite dune top. I was hesitant. Reluctant. At that time, I didn't understand that myself but I couldn't pinpoint why.

After some time had passed, I left the house one day at five in the morning. It was chilly, but according to the weather forecast, it would be sunny later. In the twilight, I climbed my favorite dune, laid out my blanket, and sat down.

I emptied my mind and focused on my breathing. Slowly, the sun came up. The sunrise was a breathtaking spectacle. Soft yellow colors with sweeps of pink and red appeared on the horizon. Calmly, I breathed on. I let my thoughts come and go, I let them pass like clouds as I had learned. I kept focusing on the question: what is my passion? Suddenly, very clearly, I envisioned it: writing. I will write a book. I have to write a book. I frowned. Gone was my meditative state. Disappointed, I stared at the beautiful sunrise. I loved writing, but a book—could I even do that? And what should it be about? I didn't know what to do with that insight at that time.

Even though I hadn't completely found myself and my passions during the retreat or on that dune tip, I did find a path. I became very much aware of what energized me and what did not. I evaluated my day daily. And, of course, I didn't immediately take action on everything or start doing things that energized me. No, I still adapted myself regularly and sometimes wanted to do something for others even though that didn't energize me directly. Aside from that, I was aware that I still didn't know exactly what my passions were. I accepted that, and that acceptance gave me peace.

Through *love me*, through this new way of looking at things, I had crossed the threshold toward a life in connection with my source. Little by little, I removed the rocks and boulders that I had pushed into my life stream. I learned to look back at my patterns and clearly came to see the bigger picture. Not that I could explain it to other people yet—I still didn't have words for that—but my life was changing. People around me mentioned that I was walking a different route.

The most interesting thing for me was that it didn't matter that I didn't know what my passions were yet, and it didn't matter if I didn't know what a different path entailed. It was about making the decision to follow my inner voice no matter what. Big changes usually start with small steps, and in my situation, I could fully attest to that.

When I discovered *love me*, I found that the people around me weren't necessarily happy with me choosing my own path. Moreover, I noticed that new behavior triggers responses. When we decide to walk our own path, the people around us are forced to deal with us differently. When we start behaving differently, they have to change too. And people don't like change. Especially when it's caused by new behavior from another person.

My niece, who had just started out as an entrepreneur, asked me if I could help her with her bookkeeping. Contrary to my usual response, I said no. She didn't take it well. After all, I did help other entrepreneurs around me with their problems. And that was exactly the problem. I had limited spare time, and through *love me* I realized that I had to learn to sometimes say no when I didn't have the time or when I preferred to spend my time on something else.

My first conscious *love-me*-no immediately led to the end of the relationship with my niece. My new behavior turned out to have consequences. Luckily, I had enough people around me who were completely fine with my new yeses and nos and who started to care more about what was good for me.

So when I noticed that some people started turning away from me or avoiding me as I gained clarity and started prioritizing my choices, I gave them the space to do so. Most of them came back, and that deepened our relationship. And if they didn't come back, I kept my course and was at peace with the idea that we both had gone our separate ways, painful as it might be. I had to *love me*.

Surrounded by my friends, acquaintances, and colleagues, I managed to get the hang of *love me* fairly well. But when I fell in love again, my fear set in. I was determined not to lose myself in a relationship this time.

ANGRY WITH THE KITE SURFER

Almost a year after divorcing the psychologist, I found myself in a new relationship, this time with a tough kite surfer. I had learned a lot from my previous relationships, and we promised each other solemnly to always keep communicating. No dirty linen in the cellar for me anymore. Such a promise is easily made, but the application sometimes becomes way too complicated.

Seemingly small things can trigger bigger things. For example, when the kite surfer told my friends that we loved arugula salad with strawberries or enjoyed watching movies, I was immediately

continued

triggered. "Speak for yourself," I would say. We weren't a we. We were he and I. Such statements felt like something was decided for me.

Or like the desktop incident that got completely out of hand. I wanted to put a link to a subtitle application that I had downloaded on my laptop's desktop so I could log in easily from my home screen. But I couldn't manage it.

"Can you help me, please?" I asked the kite surfer.

He looked over my shoulder and said: "Search through Explorer. No, not there." Impatiently, he drummed his fingers on the table. "Just let me do it. If you give me the laptop, it is easier to find."

I slid my laptop toward him, and the kite surfer started typing furiously.

"Done," he said triumphantly after a while. "And look, I arranged all your links for your convenience."

I stared at my desktop. Instead of seeing links haphazardly scattered across my desktop, the links were now neatly arranged in a list. I felt like someone had gone through my personal mail. "I only asked you to put a link for VLC on my desktop, not to reorganize my entire laptop!"

"But now you have more oversight."

"That's not the point. What were you thinking?!" His arranging my laptop felt like an invasion of my privacy. The longer I stared at my desktop, the more furious I got. "It's my laptop, and you can't just touch it like that. I don't touch your papers on your desk, do I?"

The kite surfer was taken aback by my extreme response. With a sad face, he walked away from the table and plopped on the sofa, sulking. That made me even angrier and surly. I walked to the kitchen.

Later, when I had calmed down, we were able to talk it through and investigate what this incident had done to him and me.

Talking about everything that doesn't sit right with me—no matter how big or how small, how much sense it makes or not—prevents me from throwing more dirty linen in my cellar. By speaking my truth, I clarify what matters to me, and it becomes easier for me to demand my space. With that, I also discover my sensitivities and learn how to laugh about my extreme responses.

The kite surfer and I also made some practical agreements about money. When we went out, we did it going Dutch. Later, when he officially moved in with me, we shared all our expenses. But the house was listed in my name. I went on holiday with my son or alone if I wanted to. My passions were still not completely clear to me, but I was placing fence posts to make room for continuing that journey. *Love me.*

It didn't sound romantic, of course. "You're in love and you make such specific agreements," the people around me sputtered. But I needed that.

And I think that most people fresh out of a second-choice life need that. Because it will take awhile before you are able to let go of those old habits. At least, for me it did.

Love me, and then love you.

Love me took on an even deeper meaning for me when I took part in an ayahuasca retreat in Peru[2] a few years later, in my late forties.

Ayahuasca is a tea made from leaves and roots. The native inhabitants of South America use the tea to cure diseases, to break through addictions, and to gain deep insights. The tea had a mind-expanding effect. On the internet, I had read stories from people about their visions during the ritual and the shifts it had brought about in their lives. I wanted that kind of vision too, especially because I felt I could dive a few more strokes deeper into myself. Moreover, the culture and rituals of the natives fascinated me. After an evening of googling, I found a retreat that suited the few free weeks that the kite surfer and I had.

DRUMMING SHAMANS

The kite surfer and I were part of a group of seventeen people from all over the world, and during the retreat we participated in an ayahuasca ritual three times. The rituals took place in an open maloca, a large wooden base with a fence and covered with a thatched roof, surrounded by the jet-black darkness of the evening and night of the jungle. While the shamans drummed, sang, and whistled, and the nocturnal animals made themselves heard from the jungle, we drank the tea.

On that first night, I didn't know what to expect. I lay calmly back on my mattress, wrapped in a blanket, listening to the sounds, feeling whether I noticed anything. After about ten minutes, the tea started to work. Images appeared, and I told myself to receive them calmly. After that, I was just in the vision—I had left the maloca and yet I was still there. It was easy. Radiant images alternated.

I saw myself as the center of the universe. From there, I connected with everything around me with white, yellowish, and white-blue energy channels, a radiant center that reached around and connected everything without words, without thoughts. A deep, warm feeling of peace welled up inside me. I sank into it and let myself be carried away. Then I felt a love pouring out from within myself, the stream getting faster and faster in beautiful luminous rays. It fed everything around me. That continued until I had to puke.

The side effect of the tea is that most people vomit sooner or later. In the ritual, puking means releasing toxic thoughts or emotions. You free yourself from them. I felt that way too.

The morning after the ritual, the talking stick passed around the group. The natives use the talking stick for orderly consultation. Everyone sits in a circle to express equality. The others listen without interrupting to whoever has the talking stick in his hand.

That morning, everyone said something about what they had learned from the previous evening. The kite surfer put *love me* on the table. He had received images that, for him, gave *love me* meaning. "Love your neighbor as you love yourself," came to his mind. He really lived the meaning of those words for the first time: "If you love yourself, you can love others. If you don't love yourself completely, you can't love others. *Love me* comes first. From *love me, love you* can arise."

His insight gave new meaning to my images of the center of the universe, which I connected to and which nourished everything. *Love me* was bigger than I was. I thought that was a nice thought, and my source was given a little more space to flow again.

Love me had impacted all the participants; we joked about it when we wanted to do something that wasn't on the schedule.

continued

When we arrived back home after the retreat, we received a picture from one of the participants, a physiotherapist. The first client he had treated after the Peru trip had *"I Love Me"* printed on his boxers. *Love me,* then *love you* can follow.

Love your neighbors as you love yourself. In our culture, we place a lot of emphasis on the first part: love your neighbors, and we pretend that the second part doesn't exist. How we should love ourselves is not taught in school. I myself found it hard to look in the mirror and say wholeheartedly: "I love you." I needed a lot of practice to be able to do that. Because of that retreat, I understood that if I was criticizing myself, I was also criticizing the people closest to me. The way you love yourself is how you love others.

Loving ourselves unconditionally. *Love me.* Sometimes we make a big mess out of our lives. I had made a mess out of my life sometimes. And that mess I could leave in the past with compassion and self-forgiveness. Empty out the cellars. Open your windows and doors. Live and *love me.* After that, there's *love you.* Then you'll also be able to love others unconditionally as they are.

Love me. When I finally stepped over that threshold and set out on my way, the flywheel started turning faster and faster. I did everything to find my passions. Retreats became more often, like those in Andalusia and Peru but also closer to home. I attended weekends in which I was screaming at other people as a means of meditation. Everything to be set free. To break down the dams.

With a friend I followed the Mary and Michael line, a well-known ley line on which some of Britain's most sacred sites are situated, such as the Avebury stone circles, Stonehenge, and churches dedicated to St. Michael and St. Mary (the Christian-ized earth goddess), and visited their energetic power spots.[3] Along that line, we interviewed people and made a film out of it. We sold only fifty DVDs, but that film inspired me to work on a documentary about Heiloo, a village in which one can find energetic power spots.[4] That film was broadcast on the regional broadcaster and enjoyed by many people. The interviews for the films came about spontaneously; I didn't have to put in much effort. They were small steps on my path to restoring the con-nection with my source. I had never made a documentary before, and yet it worked. It was fun and gave insight into my passion: storytelling. I decided to walk in a different direction in my spare time, in my relationships and at work. And once I got going, with trial and error, the flywheel went faster and faster. So even if you start baking cookies because you feel like it, or buy a colorful pair of shoes that you never dared to wear but find so beautiful—it doesn't matter how small the step is. Small steps can lead to big changes. They set the flywheel in motion. Until it turns so fast that it turns all by itself. *Love me* is the first step toward restoring the connection with your source.

> *Putting yourself first is not easy.* Love me *has consequences for the people around us, and shifting your course, your behavior, requires courage.* Love me *is the beginning of restoring the con-nection with our source.*
>
> *Grab a mirror and look at your own reflection. What do you feel when you say: "I love you"?*

GETTING TO KNOW YOUR OWN NATURAL QUALITIES

We are born with our own personal toolbox, our natural qualities. Recognizing, acknowledging, and embracing those natural qualities can help us restore the connection with our source. Because of our upbringing, the prevailing norms, and the people around us, we often try to be better. But we don't have to be better. It's more important that we live to our full potential, that we open those sluices and start living in connection with our source. The more we accept our natural qualities, the better we can use them, and the faster we come into contact with our source.

I found recognizing and accepting my list of natural qualities more difficult than I had thought beforehand. Good qualities also have a negative counterpart. And aside from that, my learned ideas and my feelings did not always agree. To try and bring some structure to my list, I used four kinds of entries:

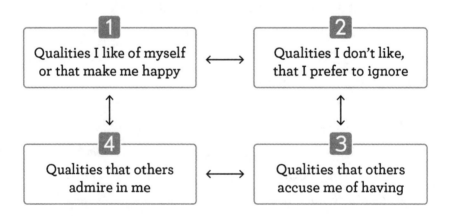

Image 5.1. My toolbox of natural qualities

I started with the qualities that I liked, followed by their negative counterpart, their not-so-pretty side. I wrote down the positive counterpart of the qualities that others accused me of having.

I found myself reliable and a connector—great qualities. The other side of those qualities is that I sometimes hurt myself with them. I find it difficult to go back on decisions, even though I want to. As a connector, I tend to look for compromises. Looking for compromises is the other side of being a connector. But I know from my childhood that compromises can also cause problems. People accused me of restlessness, fickleness. The counterpart of that is: lively, courageous, daring.

People admired my freedom and thought I was an adventurer. And the adventurer's counterpart is: restlessness, a seeker. It made me chuckle, as it was almost the same as the behavior people accused me of.

The fact that I wanted a divorce within three months of marriage may seem harsh, especially considering that I had proposed just three months earlier. On the other side of my decision to go through with the divorce, I remained true to myself. I acknowledged my mistake and took action. Jotting down these thoughts helped me gain a more comprehensive understanding of myself and learn to accept who I am. There's no inherent right or wrong when it comes to our natural qualities. They exist as they are. A perfectionist need not strive to be less of a perfectionist; it's about choosing when to harness that trait. Alternatively, we can find humor and view our behaviors with kindness. *Love me.*

Compromising often helped me in business transactions. That quality is less useful in my private life, so I don't use it that often. Similarly, I also love my adventurous character, so I accept the restlessness that accompanies that. The restlessness puts me in motion and prevents me from sleepwalking, from just going through the motions—I know that now.

In life, we sometimes do things we really can't see the good side of. Look at your behavior, even if it is bad or not so nice, and learn from it. With no judgment, simply see it, face it. The practice is incredibly enlightening. Being ruthlessly honest helps you accept yourself completely. I know that from experience.

HURT BOYS

About a year and a half after the incident with my boss at the fish packaging company, I met a boy I fell in love with at a bar. He was a few years older than me, had a motorcycle, and was a tough guy. We started dating. After a few months of kissing and touching, my boyfriend wanted to have sex with me. I also wanted that, but at the same time, I was only fifteen, and I was scared.

I had just come out of an inward phase. Still, I hadn't told my friends about the incident at the fish packaging company. Before that, an acquaintance had cornered me and touched my breasts without my permission. I also hadn't told that to anyone. In that same period, I was harassed by a boy at the frat, which led to a fight. I had defended myself, and at the frat, I was saved, but by now, I had become distant toward boys and men. And if I'm being completely honest—and I have to be—I was just a scared young girl, nervous for my first time. With my girlfriends, I giggled about sex, but I couldn't imagine what it really entailed. And there was the danger of getting pregnant. Or of my parents finding out about it.

All kinds of thoughts ran through my head, but I kept them to myself. I didn't tell my boyfriend. I came up with excuses to prevent us from having sex, but my boyfriend kept pushing in a soft and sweet way. Cornered, I chose a dramatic way out. I ended the relationship. It hurt terribly; I was still madly in love with him, but I didn't know what else to do.

To be able to break up with him, I accused my boyfriend of cheating. I knew it wasn't true, but if I shared my fears with him, I was scared he would convince me to have sex anyway. I couldn't possibly say that I wasn't in love with him anymore. So, by saying that he was cheating on me, I could run away from him crying. But the fact that my tears were caused by the pain of having to break up with him wasn't visible to him.

My boyfriend, however, didn't give up. He wanted to prove to me that he had not cheated. To push him away from me, I had to take it to another level. A day later, I kissed his best friend in his presence. Only once, because I didn't like him. The relationship was definitely over. I left behind two hurt boys.

Why am I telling you this, you might wonder?

I am telling you this because it is difficult to be ruthlessly honest with yourself, while that is the biggest gift you can give yourself.

Admitting that I behaved badly makes me a better person. It makes me more real. I don't like facing this kind of behavior, but it helps me understand that it is essential to speak up in a relationship, no matter how difficult that can be. It helps me be more courageous in that area of my life.

continued

> Nowadays, I understand that we both have a light and a dark side, like yin and yang. Without a dark side, we aren't able to shine. If we only have a light side, we miss being grounded with our roots in the dark earth. How can we be compassionate toward others if we are not grounded? It is high time that I say goodbye to my dirty linen syndrome so I can speak up whenever needed.

Care for a Little Exercise?

Gaining insight into our inherent qualities forms a solid foundation for reestablishing our connection with the source. Take a moment to complete the chart in Appendix A for yourself. Appendix A includes a blank chart and a comprehensive list of qualities that encompass both the positive and negative aspects of each quality. This list can aid you in identifying your own qualities, although it is ultimately a tool, and your personal intuition should guide you. Reflecting on the qualities we appreciate and those we dislike about ourselves has assisted me in recognizing the childhood interests that continue to manifest in my work and how I choose to spend my leisure time. These interests serve as valuable indicators. In Breezand, I learned to ride a bicycle, and for me, cycling represented adventure. It allowed me to traverse long distances and explore uncharted worlds. In my perception, cycling had little to do with being sporty but everything to do with embracing adventure.

It also helped me reflect on the bad situations I found myself in. How did I end up there? What quality made sure things escalated, were covered up, or thrown in the cellar? I thought about my studies, my professions. Which qualities matched those? What qualities have I benefited from?

With the qualities that others assigned to me, I filled in those that were regularly pointed out to me. What stories do our parents or our siblings often tell about us? Which qualities accompany those stories? For what kinds of things do our colleagues ask us for help, and which issues come forward in our final reports? How do our friends see us?

Strive for utmost honesty as you complete your chart. Remember, there are no inherently good or bad qualities. Optimism guides us through challenging moments, while pessimism safeguards us from venturing into unnecessary risks. A knack for improvisation proves invaluable during emergencies, but when organizing medications, we require our sense of structure or perfectionism.

~~~

Everyone is unique, adds a unique contribution to our existence, and shapes it with his or her natural qualities. There are millions of combinations, maybe even billions or endless combinations. And existence needs all of those combinations.

> *Our natural qualities don't see good or bad. Having insight into your qualities is a good foundation for restoring the connection with your source. It provides us with a choice. It helps us to accept ourselves fully.*
>
> *What does your list with natural qualities look like?*

PATTERNS AND ROUTINES

Everyone has patterns and routines, and that is a good thing. A pattern helps to make life more manageable. Routines make sure that we don't have to think about everything. It's similar to driving a car: We don't have to think about where the blinker is, and if a traffic light turns red, we automatically hit the brake. Routines help to make it possible for us to focus completely on the traffic.

Patterns are nothing more than automatic responses to situations we encounter. Some patterns are innocent; they support us. Some patterns are destructive. Sometimes, we respond in a way that doesn't suit us. It is learned behavior that is not ours, but it belongs to our parents, siblings, school, employer, colleagues, or friends. We have translated these customs into patterns that, in turn, lead to roles.

In particular, patterns that don't serve us but systematically undermine us in a subtle way are often difficult to spot. Recognizing the patterns, roles, and routines that do or don't help us is necessary preliminary work to restoring the connection with your source.

SECOND IN COMMAND

Because I am often asked by management or boards of companies and institutions to help a department or business unit to a more professional level, I had convinced myself that I worked best as second in command, as a helper to the management or board. This pattern probably originated from my ability as a connector. As a connector,

I automatically sense during the first contact whether what I say or do comes across the right way to the other person. If the other doesn't respond well, I automatically adjust my behavior. Then, I try to use different words or compromise more with the other person's direction.

It's an excellent pattern for a connector, but it's undermining if this pattern always automatically sets in. For me, that leads to an unconscious second-in-command role. I envisioned myself in those days as the driving force behind the CEO or the manager. Even as interim manager, I was second in command to the board of CEOs or shareholders. This way, I didn't see myself correctly. I hurt myself sometimes; *love me* wasn't present enough. With the second-in-command vision, I made myself smaller than necessary, pushing measures of which I instinctively knew there had to be better routes.

And I kept comparing. Unconsciously. When there is a second, there is also a first or a third. In doing so, I created a distance in working relationships. Comparison is at odds with inclusiveness. After I understood the pattern, my role perception changed. My leadership became more authentic, gave me more satisfaction, and deepened my working relationships. I came closer to myself, which, in turn, improved my performance.

One person may have had greater opportunities to live from their source during childhood compared to another. Particularly in families with a lot of activity, it becomes challenging to maintain that connection to your source. Survival mechanisms are triggered. As adults, we often carry these mechanisms and the accompanying patterns with us, unaware that we even possess them. These patterns served us well in times of need, and we continue to carry them without much conscious awareness.

When I quit school, there was a high level of youth unemployment. I would be lucky if I was even able to find a job. I didn't care what kind of job. I found a full-time job at a butchery at a supermarket. Fine by me.

Shortly after I got my own place, I needed to make ends meet to pay the rent and the groceries. The job as a typist at the municipality was a godsend. It paid one and a half times as much as working at a store. I earned the money that I needed.

It became a habit to do what must be done without asking myself if this was really what I wanted to do. Not that I was unhappy at that time. I had wonderful moments with friends. The job was fine, and the colleagues were fine, too. The job was not necessarily one I loved getting out of bed for in the morning, but it was new. And new was interesting to me. Every time I entered a world that I didn't know, I could go and explore. Living according to my source could wait (in those days, I didn't know about my source or living according to it). I was alive and discovered how the outside world worked. I was independent.

Every time I started something new or got into a new relationship, I felt fully alive. For a while, this adventure was enough for me, but soon my soul started stirring. I had to do something about this pattern of "doing what I thought I had to do" without asking myself if that was really what I wanted.

Sometimes, we only recognize a pattern when we look back. When life starts talking back louder and louder, we often discover some unhealthy patterns and roles that make us invisible and obfuscated.

CHANGING MY PATTERNS

For a long time, I hopped from one relationship into another without understanding that the only way to have a sustainable relationship was to reconnect with my source and to myself.

The same was true for my job. I worked for several employers and also started my own business. Allegedly, I had a career. I got jobs and projects that required more responsibility. I became a manager, executed strategy assignments, and helped organizations solve their debts. But in the meantime, I had no idea what actually made me happy. I thought I was doing very well. And always something new came my way, something new to discover, to fathom. All were distractions, so the connection with my source had to wait.

I kept throwing alarming thoughts, uncomfortable feelings, and unfulfilled desires in the cellar, and in doing so, I kept them hidden from myself. Unwillingly, I was fooling myself.

In hindsight, I was mostly shocked by my first marriage. I got married to control my restlessness. I hadn't even come up with my alleged fear of commitment myself. I wish someone had said to me: "Hey, what do you think you're doing? You're only holding on to a second-choice life more and more."

But, of course, no one did that. Our marriage plans were met with joy and enthusiasm by my friends. No one likes restlessness; everyone loves the fairy tale. And I was living my second-choice life as if it was the best life I had ever had. Until the pressure became too much and life started screaming in my face.

Automatic patterns can be caused by our qualities but usually derive from our childhood, culture, and the people we deal with.

My family attached a lot of value to thriftiness, home ownership, and a stable employer. Of course, as a teenager, I tried to behave according to the customs of my family. When I started earning good money, I opened a special savings account like my brothers and my oldest sister. With this savings account, as a teenager/young adult, you received a 10 percent premium on the savings balance in the end (if you left the account untouched) from the government. I grew up in a thrifty family, and my dad was thrilled that I had opened a savings account. However, my list of natural qualities says I am adventurous, so I didn't manage to get to the finish line. Not by a long shot. I soon withdrew the money to go on a camping trip with friends from the pub—with my father's bitter disbelief as a premium.

When we do something that is against our nature, it doesn't work. We will never succeed. We won't even reach mediocracy. At most, we burn ourselves out.

Patterns change over time. When we stay true to ourselves, we say goodbye to the patterns that no longer serve us and instead develop new ones. Through new relationships, through changes in our jobs or studies, our patterns can change and, with that, our roles.

When I worked in paid employment, I undertook many hobbies in my spare time. I tried to earn as much money as possible in the least amount of time—fun work or not, I didn't care that much, and outside of work, I tried to learn, discover, and travel as much as possible. That pattern has changed. Now, I want my job to have those aspects too.

Some patterns are good to keep. Every morning, I eat my

coconut yogurt with seeds, nuts, and fresh fruit. When I stay at a hotel, I find it difficult when they don't serve yogurt. Eating yogurt for breakfast is a deeply ingrained pattern.

Some deeply ingrained patterns undermine us. Sometimes, it can take awhile for us to see them. But, once detected, we want to say goodbye to them, but changing a pattern is not always that simple. Look at the people who have trouble quitting smoking. The physical addiction is gone within a week, but the ingrained pattern makes quitting difficult. I myself used to smoke. At parties at our house, my parents served nuts and cheese cubes as well as cigarettes and cigars in tiny glasses on the table. Smoking was associated with comfort, coziness, togetherness. Later in high school, you were only cool when you smoked, and everybody smoked in bars. The cigarette was my best friend in all circumstances: at fun events, but also when I was down. Breaking that pattern cost me months, and still, after not smoking for twenty years, I sometimes feel like an ex-smoker.

~~~

I can only change a pattern or take a different direction when I really want it and when I try to make a deal with myself. I don't exchange it for a similar pattern, but I hold on and take a different route. And I stick to it for at least a month.

I left the second-in-command pattern behind by looking at what drove me daily, exchanging an old pattern for a new way of think-ing. In doing so, I didn't give in to that old pattern anymore, and over time, that changed my actions. My train of thought changed; my brain started making different connections and sought new paths. For example, I suppressed my tendency, my automatic pat-tern, to focus as much as possible on the general manager or senior management I worked for and follow his or her decision-making. I forced myself to reconsider when dealing with certain issues. As a result, I took charge more often, considered the route that seemed best to me, then made the decision myself and inquired when necessary. This eliminated the idea of being second in command.

Will and perseverance are necessary for changing any pattern. Experts say we should keep that up for at least a month. If we can keep it up for that amount of time, the chances are that we can actually leave the pattern behind us. And with some patterns, we will be stuck forever. Then, you have to keep paying attention. Just like I will always be an ex-smoker.

Forced patterns and the resulting roles don't serve us. In the end, we have no idea what the purpose of our lives is or where our real passions lie. We become completely cut off from the source. We feel dulled down from caring so much about other people's opinions that we run out of energy. Or we waste all our energy suppressing our inner restlessness, withdraw, don't let anyone get close to us, or react unusually fiercely to keep people at a distance. We can't help it. Behind our dams, we are powerless, closed off.

Invisible patterns that control us in the background and are not easily noticeable are the hardest to break. There's only one remedy: As soon as I become aware of an undermining pattern, I have to want to change that pattern.

Patterns that don't serve us—we can see them as dams in our life streams. They block our natural flow, sending us onto the wrong path or keeping us stuck on the shore.
Which pattern would you like to break?

ARE YOU DREAMING OR ARE YOU BEING DREAMED?

Inventions such as the wheel were made in different places around the world during the same period with no mutual contact between the inventors.[5] Information exchange via the telephone, internet, or other data connections did not yet exist; the ideas about the invention seemed to be lingering in the air, conveyed by an energy that seemed to find its way from one side of the world to the other—the force of thoughts. Just like people who think of each other and then call each other at the same time.

Many signs indicate that we are connected. And not only with each other, but also with the animals, the plants, the mountains, the sea, the earth, the stars, the sun, the moon, the universe. This connection is reflected in all kinds of religions and old traditions; system therapies are based on it, and scientists analyze it as a phenomenon, especially in quantum physics.

Some people are focused on the "law of attraction." This law states that when you want something really bad and you think about it and visualize that it is already there, the universe will put it on your path.

Are you being dreamed is inspired by a combination of the law of attraction and the books of Jamie Sams,[6] who writes about the old spiritualities of Native Americans, whose ancestors were part of the Cherokee and Seneca tribes. In her books, Sams writes about the tradition of the Choctaws in which dreams are considered valuable, and the tribe interprets different kinds of dreams. *Being dreamed* is being the answer to someone else's dream.

Are you dreaming evolves around our own dream, our own wish. When a dream really connects with our inner world, when we want something really bad and visualize it—there's a chance that it will manifest itself. As a child, I wished with all my heart that we would leave Breezand. Later, I wondered if the export prices plummeted because of that, which is why we moved. Afterward, I even felt a little guilty about it, as I hadn't wished for low export prices for my father.

Dreams help us on our path. Dreams lead to a vision. I am not necessarily referring to the dreams we have at night while we sleep. Those can also be enlightening, but in this case, it's all about the dreams we have about how we would like to live our lives, what we would like to achieve, what we would like to do. Keep in mind that the universe has its own plan. Our dreams don't always manifest themselves in the way or form that we were expecting.

IN THE LATTER DAYS WITH THE PSYCHOLOGIST

In the waning of my relationship with the psychologist, I wanted to move to a cheaper place. I had given up the idea that he would start earning his share of the deal, and I couldn't cope anymore. His interest in photography, the new way for him to start earning money, was fading already, and he was doubting whether he wanted to make a profession out of it. If I had been more realistic, I could have predicted this outcome. But it didn't matter anymore.

It had become clear to me that I had to make choices for myself. What did I want? Divorce him or continue like this for a while? I had derailed my part in the relationship so much that I doubted I could make it work again. And I wasn't sure either if I wanted it to work. I became more restless by the day, and the relationship became more uncomfortable. But I had no doubt that I wanted to find a cheaper place to live, which wasn't easy in Bergen.

The cosmos helped me a little. Acquaintances of my husband lived in free-sector housing and were planning to move. Their rent was half of what we paid for our detached house. They invited us over to check the place out. It was a corner house with a lovely garden, and we immediately said yes. The landlord agreed to it, and suddenly, in a month and a half, I would have the cheaper house that I wanted so badly.

This cheaper house also offered a way out. I hardly dared to think about it. I woke up one night in the middle of the night, slipped out of bed, and went downstairs. Through the window, I watched the soft light of the waxing crescent moon. What did I want? Even though I had wished for a cheaper house to reduce our living costs, this also offered the opportunity to get a divorce. As the main breadwinner, I definitely had to pay for both houses, which was now possible with this new house. I snuggled up in my chair, and my thoughts continued in circles. After a while, I felt cold. The moon was still shining its soft light—no wink or flickering or the man in the moon giving me any sign.

I quietly slipped upstairs again and lay down on the edge of the bed as far as possible from my husband. I needed space, a place of my own. That was my true dream.

That place turned out not to be it, but it made my own place possible. Right before we moved from the detached house, we separated. The psychologist moved into the cheaper house, and

continued

after a few temporary holiday homes, I found an apartment over a shop in Bergen. It was good for our son and our co-parenting if we could both live in Bergen. And I was ready to start shaping my own life.

Are you being dreamed evolves around the idea that another person is dreaming of you as a solution to a problem or a part of his or her personal wish. Being dreamed of has two sides. One side gives us the opportunity to explore terrains where we never would have gone without the other person.

A TRIP TO EGYPT

A yoga teacher from Bergen had made a beautiful trip to Egypt— seven days of floating on the Red Sea, swimming with wild dolphins, snorkeling along coral reefs, and enjoying the silent and dark starry night sky in the middle of the sea. Excited, she returned from her trip and wanted to do the same trip again with a group of women that she knew.

Personally, I am more of a hiker, and I love roaming around in nature, in the mountains, along cliffs, and along pilgrims' paths, so such a trip wasn't necessarily at the top of my bucket list, but swimming with dolphins did speak to me. So I decided to attend the information meeting.

The yoga teacher's excitement was contagious. Even though I had some second thoughts, such as whether we would be disturbing the dolphins, I envisioned myself lying on the deck of the boat, being able to swim at any time of the day, in the middle of the sea, surrounded by coral reefs and dolphins. It seemed like a fairy tale. She assured me that it was local and respectful tourism, that the dolphins only showed up when they felt like it. So after a few days of thinking it over, I said yes. A few months later, I traveled to Egypt with a group of women.

For a whole week, we were part of the yoga teacher's dream who had organized the whole venture. The trip turned out to be amazing, one that brought me new friendships. I also loved getting close to the wonderful creatures who inspired me to a whole different heart frequency, who awakened the playfulness in me. I was being dreamed and let myself be dreamed.

By being part of the path of the dreamer for a week, I got to know the energy of the dolphins; it turned out to be an enrichment that I could take along with me on my path. Moreover, the trip led to a deepening of my own dreams. The book I had envisioned that day on the dune top started taking shape in my head.

Aside from the unknown horizons, there is also a downside to being dreamed. We can unknowingly drift from our own paths onto the path of another by being dreamed, a path that we mistakenly think of as our own. Especially when we are living a second-choice life, it is difficult to be dreamed. When we are not exactly sure of our own deep passions and goals and are being dreamed, we quickly tend to follow. But is that really our own path: are you dreaming, or are you being dreamed?

I WASN'T PAYING ATTENTION

In my life, I have walked paths that were not meant for me, but in hindsight, I find it difficult to say that's the moment I was being dreamed. I spot that sooner with other people.

In my job as an entrepreneur, I was being dreamed once or twice. Before I would finish a project, I got offered a new one. My essential attitude was: "That's great, the cosmos is really taking care of me." I arranged a meeting, found out what the company expected of me, and told them what I could do for them. If there was a mutual connection, we would make an appointment, and I would start working on the project.

And sometimes, during that process, it turned out that I wasn't always careful enough toward myself. So it happened that after a merger of two branches, I ended up with the same company on a new project. I had to design a blueprint of processes that could then be applied nationally. According to the client, I had gained extensive knowledge of the product and service package in the merger process, and they liked my working method.

It was a time of crisis; many of my colleagues had no work, so it confirmed to me that the cosmos was taking good care of me. But I hadn't consulted my feelings sufficiently while I happily started working on the new project. And I paid the price for that. Of course, I include the refinement or renewal of processes in my daily work, but that is not the same as being a legitimate process designer and writer.

Being very structured or organized is not necessarily on top of my list of natural qualities, so for three months, I toiled, doubted myself, and lay awake at night because the plans kept swirling through my mind. Eventually, I was able to deliver that blueprint, but those three months cost me over six months of energy.

I was being dreamed, and I didn't pay enough attention.

Dreaming and Hope

Dreams are not to be confused with hope. Unmani, a teacher in nonduality, was certain in her vision of hope. She said: "Hope is one of the worst things there is. Hope takes you away from the now."[7] Hope makes you live in a fantasy world. You don't confront the threat head-on; therefore, you cannot coincide with the whole.

With dreams, we redesign our path. By dreaming, we see where we could go to, where the law of attraction can find us. Sometimes hope is similar to dreaming, but hope in the form of "I have doubts and I hope I will succeed," on the other hand, is a binding energy. During my search, I noticed that with hoping, I fell back into a second-choice life and drifted away from my connection with my source, while dreaming made me more active and feel more alive.

With newly gained respect, I thought back to Martin Luther King's speech: "I have a dream." He had chosen his words well. If he had said at that moment, "I hope that" instead of "I have a dream," his speech probably wouldn't have been as impressive. Hope often sounds less powerful, like it takes someone else or better conditions to get where you want to go. Dreaming, on the other hand, has the action of the dreamer in it, which bystanders can follow.

I learned that dreaming provides us with energy in the now. Just like trust does. Without dreaming and trusting, we can sink into our own swamp. When I visualize the energy of dreaming, I see myself emerging from my swamp with confidence. I dream of the riverbank where I lie in the fresh green grass. The dew tickles my face. The sun warms it. That's where I want to go.

On my path to restoring the connection with the source, I have replaced hope with dreaming and trusting. I was not *hoping* to write this book. I wasn't *hoping* I could do it. I *dreamed* of what my book would look like. I relied on my creativity, agility, and flexibility. I longed for the manifestation of the book.

I find that dreaming gives me vision and direction. With hoping, I lose control. There is no active direction. Hope makes me weary and lazy. I do hope, but what can I do about it? Unintentionally, I was being dreamed more often by hoping. Keep on dreaming and trusting. I asked myself: am I hoping for a different life or, like Martin Luther King, am I having a dream and am I confident in the steps I am taking? Am I doing what needs to be done? Small steps lead to big changes.

Are you dreaming or are you being dreamed? When you are living a second-choice life, you have to be careful with being dreamed because we tend to think of the path of the other as our own. Being able to make a distinction between dreaming and being dreamed has helped me on my way to restoring the connection with my source.

Are you dreaming or are you being dreamed? If you're able to make this distinction, you have a choice. You can explore new horizons without limitations and you can still see your own path.

Do you draw your own plan or are you a confluence of events?

WHO'S TALKING NOW?

While searching for who I am, my passions, and how I keep being connected to my source, I have regularly spent weekends, retreats, and days with Jan van Delden,[8] an Advaita teacher. Advaita is a belief in nonduality, the vision that all is one. I think van Delden is a gifted storyteller, and he supports his story with chairs (van Delden's chairs), Teletubby dolls, and other props.

From him and from the Buddhists, I learned about the 108 voices on my shoulders. Or rather: the 108 tiny Theas on my shoulders—54 characters on the right side and 54 on the left, none of which are the true me. And whether there are exactly 108? I didn't count them. The number 108 is a sacred number in Buddhism (and in other traditions and religions). For example, Buddha would have asked himself 108 questions, man must resist 108 worldly temptations to reach Nirvana, and so there are several other examples for the number 108.

The voices have nothing to do with the source or a being, but they do belong to us. They are inseparable, always present. We have grown fond of some of the voices or characters, and others we loathe. But we can't get rid of them. What we can do is ask ourselves: "Who's talking now?" And we can also bypass the voices, as van Delden beautifully depicts. The latter takes some practice, but bypassing them brings us closer to the source.

How does this work? When we make a decision about something, there are always voices that tell us: "Is that really wise? Wouldn't it be better to . . . ?" I wanted to buy a new car while my current car was only two-and-a-half years old. Normally, I trade in my cars after four years. That time frame is business-wise; with four years, the car remains reliable and representative. To trade in a "younger" car was therefore accompanied by the following positive and negative voices.

THE ELECTRIC CAR

The kite surfer wanted a new lease car, and his employer wanted it to be a sustainable one. His search had led to two electric cars, and he wanted to know my opinion about them.

We made several test drives. Driving in an electric car was an epiphany for me. Aside from its sustainability, it also drove smoothly, involved no clutching when you're stuck in traffic, was wonderfully silent, and had an action radius like I'd never seen before. I wanted one too!

The two cars we tried out were too big for me, but there was also a smaller type on display in the showroom, which was entirely to my taste with a white steering wheel and dashboard. That car made me happy. Plus it came with only an 8 percent addition (yearly vehicle tax)[9] instead of the 22 percent I had to pay for my regular car, and a nice discount because it was the previous year's model. The salesperson tempted me to make a test drive, and I was sold.

Then, the voices in my head started talking.

"Those four years haven't passed yet," said strict Thea.

The exuberant Thea: "If you like it, just take it."

"That car might be cheaper in taxes, but it is probably much more expensive due to the depreciation," pessimistic Thea warned me.

"You don't need a new car, it's a waste of money," frugal Thea said.

Commercial Thea: "You'll probably leave a better impression with your clients with an electric car than with that tiny car you have now."

Incidentally, the latter was true. Everywhere I went, I was criticized for my tiny red petrol car: it didn't suit my work position, I drove long distances, it was too small, and so on.

In an attempt to briefly silence the voices, I asked about the trade-in value of my current car. The first calculation I found too low, but the salesperson could come up with a better offer if I came by the store with my car.

"I'll think about it," I told him.

When I arrived home, the little characters on my shoulders went wild. They kept on talking and talking about the pros and cons. The sense and non-sense of an electric car. The approval and disapproval of trading in such a relatively new car. Sustainable versus petrol car.

The next morning, I woke up and asked myself: "Who is talking today? Is that me or are those my characters?" I tried to bypass

continued

them. I tried buttering them up: "Yes, you are completely right. I'll be careful, calculate it well, I won't be fooled." They eventually fell silent.

As I'm writing this, my new electric car will be delivered in two weeks.

Asking yourself the question: "Who's talking now?" followed by bypassing those characters is an excellent strategy to stay true to yourself. By going along with the voices or characters, we have more chance of bypassing them. As van Delden said: "The best way to bypass your characters is by sucking up to them, to fight them by buttering them up." I was buttering up my frugal Thea by thanking her for warning me. Moreover, I told her that driving electric was cheaper per year because of the lower taxes and the low maintenance costs in comparison to the petrol car. I shut down exuberant Thea by saying that I loved her enthusiasm. I reassured strict Thea by saying that she was completely right and that because of her remarks, I had thought it through better. Buttering up is actually quite similar to not trying to fight teenagers but instead trying to get on their good side. We take a different approach.

When we can bypass the characters, we get an answer from our source or soul. This answer can look like talking but is usually distinguishable from the voices by the different energy with which the answer comes. It often feels like a calm knowing, an intuition; your mind becomes silent. Especially concerning decisions where much is at stake, it is good to get in touch with the source.

With a decision made in connection with our source, we stand stronger—even if our decision deeply influences others, our family, or our culture. Then we know how to stay calm in those situations because the decision feels right to us.

For instance, when the psychologist and I broke up while we had a child together, suppose I hadn't made that decision in connection with my source. In that case, I'm not sure if I could have handled the flood of blame, emotions, and well-intentioned advice that I received from my environment and from my own voices. With decisions like that, it suddenly became essential that I had learned to bypass the characters on my shoulders.

Our voices also talk to people who are not there. We sometimes have whole conversations with partners, friends, colleagues, and managers, and our characters fill in the answers and arguments of those people. It all happens in our heads. Although it is an inner dialogue based on assumptions about the other person's reaction and not on facts, we often take the imaginary discussion extremely seriously. Based on those conversations, we take certain positions and form an opinion, which can hinder us in the conversation with the other person. These characters can also be bypassed when we keep being alert.

The characters and voices are simply part of us. See them and acknowledge them so you learn to recognize them faster. For example, some of my voices speak louder than others—the tough Thea, the carpe diem Thea, the frugal Thea, Thea the mother. For me, they are all called Thea, but I also know people who assign different names to them.

~~~

I love my different characters; I laugh with them, cry with them, but I don't let them decide. Connecting with our source allows us to bypass the characters and voices on our shoulders.

> *Who's talking now? There are 108 voices on our shoulders, 54 on the light side and 54 on the dark side. None of them is you. Which characters do you have on your shoulders? What are they telling you?*

A SUMMARY OF THE PRELIMINARY WORK

The preliminary work is perhaps the hardest part. Just as clearing the soil of weeds and shaking it loose before planting is a lot of work, so is getting to know ourselves, truly seeing ourselves, and learning to love ourselves.

With *love me*, we put the first spade in the ground. We loosen the ground by honoring ourselves and doing what is important to us. Putting ourselves first is not the same as being self-centered. If we don't care for ourselves, we also can't be there for others.

We remove the weeds from our garden by getting to know our natural qualities. We clean out our toolbox, remove what is not ours, and get rid of what doesn't suit us. We become more real when we recognize and embrace our natural traits and talents. There is no need to improve ourselves, to behave differently than we are, and to teach ourselves something we were not meant to do. We are good the way we are.

Working the soil does not end with loosening and weeding the top layer. Deeper into the soil, hard layers may make it difficult for roots to grow and prevent the water from sinking in, resulting in rotting roots. And just as we must forcefully stir up these hard layers in the soil before planting, so we must be determined to break the patterns and roles that undermine us.

Learning to distinguish between *dreaming* and *being dreamed* helps us find our own path, just as we create a good breeding ground by adding organic material to the loosened and airy soil. Through *dreaming* and trusting, we lay the foundation for a manifestation from the source. *Being dreamed* can sometimes provide a new fertile ground, but it can also mean that we unwittingly start walking someone else's path. As fertilization for the soil, it also pays to get to know the voices on our shoulders and learn to bypass them so we can hear the answer from the source. With this preliminary work, we have cleared the soil of weeds, loosened and aired it, and provided it with nutrients. We can start planting now!

Chapter 6

THE PATH TOWARD RESTORING THE CONNECTION WITH YOUR SOURCE

T he preliminary work is done, we have crossed the threshold, and now we can start planting.

Restoring the connection with your source is a process; the path is personal. The steps, the choices, and the direction can differ for every individual. But what applies to everyone is that the process starts by making the decision to live according to our source.

This chapter provides pointers to restore the connection with the source.

OPEN YOURSELF TO THE SOURCE

When I speak about the source, I always think of the poem "De Drie Wonderlijkste Woorden" ("The Three Most Wonderful Words") by

Wisława Szymborska.[1] "When I look for the source, with every step it leads me further away from it," she might have said if she had included the source in her poem.

When we're restoring the connection with the source, we don't have to look for it because the source is already there. The source is always present, but we have lost contact with it. We can regain contact with the source by removing all the barriers that enclose the source, preventing the source from flowing, and then opening ourselves up to what the source has in store for us.

Intuitively, we know that there is a source that feeds us, a soul that seeks fulfillment. We feel it. We know when we act or react according to our source, but we can't explain it. I have learned that if we open ourselves to the source, life will start flowing naturally. Without building thresholds and dams, the source will flow freely. Our need to act comes from the source through our feelings, our intuition, or thoughts that just come to mind. We get a hunch, in a flash we can clearly envision it, or we suddenly know what to do. The thoughts can be small or big.

The source is always there and gives us a push in the right direction when we need it.

TWO DEER

I wondered: what happens when I surrender and start following life, following the source? I wanted to experience that to the fullest, to follow what popped up in me and act on what the situation needed. I called that experiment: "follow the-force-that-knows-the-way."

I had just finished a project and took a few months off to start my experiment in peace. It was January, cold, and the woods in Bergen were hibernating.

I had attended meetings in Amsterdam by Rupert Spira, and on the internet, I saw that he was organizing a retreat in San Francisco in February. Without questioning myself—bypassing my tiny Theas, the voices who all had their own opinions—I booked a trip for three weeks to the United States. The idea popped up in me, and I acted on it. I followed the-force-that-knows-the-way.

My son and the kite surfer supported me, but other people in my surroundings were skeptical. "Three weeks by yourself? Just leaving your child with your partner [the kite surfer] for a week and then another week at his father's [the psychologist]? What do you think you'll find there?" But I wasn't looking to find something there. I just followed the-force-that-knows-the-way. Nothing more, nothing less. And that force put me on a plane to San Francisco.

In San Francisco, it was easy to follow the-force-that-knows-the-way. I loved roaming around the city, cycling over the Golden Gate Bridge, and hiking along the bay. After spending a few days in the city, it was time for Rupert Spira's retreat.[2]

I immersed myself in lessons about nonduality and meditations with like-minded people. During that retreat, I met Carrie, my soul sister. A quiet woman, a bit taller and a few years older than I was, she liked to pose hard-hitting questions in the middle of a conversation or discussion. I noticed her being just as comfortable doing that in both large and smaller groups. And then she kindly laughed away the discomfort in the group. I felt my heart melt. Unconditional love, I felt for her. Without wasting any words, we

continued

made a pact and became soul mates for life. Life was taking an upward turn for me.

After the retreat, the-force-that-knows-the-way had decided to go to Arizona. I would fly from San Francisco to Phoenix, rent a car there, and drive to Angel Valley, where I had rented a cabin for a week. Angel Valley is situated in the rugged wilderness, a fifteen-minute drive from Sedona. The legendary red rocks and Native American tribes like the Hopi, Navajo, and Apache that had lived in the region really spoke to me. I wanted to feel what such a rugged environment would do to me. I admired the culture of the natives, the wisdom of the Hopi, the living-in-harmony-with-nature lifestyle of the Navajo. At the same time, I could imagine that the rituals had inflicted a lot of pain on some tribe members. The rules were quite strict. If you didn't comply with the norms of a tribe, you could be shunned.

A few days in advance, I googled Angel Valley to explore some hiking trails in the area. Reports appeared about pending lawsuits that ended a little over a year earlier because of a sweat lodge ceremony. During that ceremony, people had died. The ceremony had been performed by a host organization, but Angel Valley was held jointly liable. People stayed away, and the lawsuits almost brought Angel Valley to bankruptcy, according to the reports. Death and lawsuits—I had not imagined that for my paradise between the red rocks. Was this the right place to continue my experiment?

I started doubting, and the day before I would get on the plane, I became ill and feverish. It felt like a heavy cold. My tiny Theas took the upper hand and said that I could not fly like that. I had to cancel Angel Valley. I emailed the owners, and they responded with a nice message. It was no problem that I wasn't able to come. If this was the situation, the owner said it had to be that way. If my situation would change anytime soon, I was certainly welcome to join. They charged no cancellation costs, even though they had the right to charge me, and exerted no pressure to join anyway.

That message shook me up. I wasn't putting enough faith in the-force-that-knows-the-way and had listened too much to the Thea voices. I was only working on this experiment for a couple of weeks and I was already debating it. Did I want to take back my own life (the voices, the characters) and base my choices on that instead of following the herd?

I reconsidered my decision and left the outcome to the-force-that-knows-the-way. My soul sister gave me all kinds of medications against the flu. And I kept telling myself: if I stayed sick, then that was just meant to be, but if I could get on that plane, then that was meant to be. The next morning, I had recovered and I could start my journey.

Angel Valley turned out to be paradise. The serenity, atmosphere, mountain streams, and hills around the park were exactly what I needed. One other guest, a guy from Switzerland, had been coming there two weeks a year for years and had not been deterred by all the stories. It created a bond, and I was happy to be there and glad that I had followed the-force-that-knows-the-way.

On a beautiful sunny day, I was hiking along a path surrounded by trees and red rocks. There were no other hikers, I didn't know where the path would end, but I was clearly following a trail. After a few kilometers, the path ended at a solitary high rock, and on

continued

that rock a man sat playing the flute. I climbed up using the carved stepping stones and enjoyed the view. The flute player, small and slender, his gray hair tied together with a simple string, seated in baggy trousers, was completely absorbed by his playing and did not seem to notice me. I carefully stayed well away from him so as not to disturb him. After a while, he stopped playing and came to me. In his hand, he held a heart carved from a red rock.

"This is for you," he said. "Spread your love all over the world."

It was a wonderful encounter. It seemed like our auras melted together, and for a few seconds, we were one. Tears welled up in my eyes. Hesitantly, I took the heart from him. It felt like a great responsibility, and I wasn't sure if I could carry it. The flute player nodded encouragingly.

The rock turned out to be a sacred place for the Native Americans, a place where their descendants still came to pay their respects, and the flute player was one of them.

A few days later, I wanted to climb the hill next to Angel Valley. There were no paths there, but the summit really appealed to me. I had been looking at that hill for days, and I was curious about the view from that top. I waded across the river and started the climb. Less than a third of the way up the hill, I got completely stuck. The right flank was too steep, and I could not find a way through the thorny vegetation on the other side.

Suddenly I saw two deer. They looked at me and seemed to be calling me. I moved toward them one step at a time among the spiky plants and began following them. So I found a way through the thorny bushes and managed to reach the top. Later, the owner of Angel Valley said they hadn't seen any deer in over a year.

During that week at Angel Valley, I learned that the source never led me astray. The source pushed me to the top and helped me reach it.

To experiment with opening yourself up to the source, to follow the-force-that-knows-the-way, it is not necessary to travel to Angel Valley. When I got home, I noticed plenty of moments to practice in everyday life.

It sometimes happens to me that I dread an appointment that I previously made with friends or acquaintances. My agenda has been too full, the appointment no longer suits me because, for example, I am in a writing flow, or the need to be alone is too strong. Previously, I could worry terribly about that. Now, I leave that to the source. Sometimes, such an appointment simply expires; the other person is suddenly unable to attend or is ill. Sometimes I cancel, but not with all kinds of reasons (fabrications of the 108 characters) or a thousand excuses. I tell the other person how it feels for me. Sometimes I just go, and it turns out to be a lot of fun. I meet someone who makes me feel glad that I didn't miss out on this event, or I find out why a certain party is not suitable for me (a lesson for next time).

The acceptance that the source flows as it flows, that life goes as it goes, gives me inner peace. Those small steps, such as experimenting with my appointments, get me into the flow. It is no longer about the predetermined liking or disliking, about the pleasant or unpleasant. I follow the stream.

We restore the connection with the source by opening up, and that takes practice. Just as I accepted that the source flows as it flows with my appointments. Or if someone asks you a question, take a moment to feel instead of answering immediately. Choose a Sunday or another day to spend by yourself and follow what comes to mind that day. If you want to do something crazy (in the eyes of your little voices), just do it. If you don't want to do anything at all, that's fine. Follow what is going on within yourself that day—your thoughts, your feelings, your intuition. Let the road unfold that day, even if it feels uncomfortable. We humans are used to not following a path but pursuing a result, a goal. But results and what wants to manifest through the source are different. The result is devised by the 108 characters, provided by the environment and inspired by our ingrained convictions. By listening too much to those kinds of signs, we look for ways instead of letting the way find us.

Osho tells us: "All private goals are neurotic. The essential human comes to know, to feel, 'I am not separate from the whole, and there is no need to search for any destiny on my own. Things happen, the world is moving. . . . There is no need for me to make any struggle, any effort; is no need for me to fight for anything. I can relax and be.' The essential man is not a doer. The accidental man is a doer. The accidental man is, of course, then in anxiety, tension, stress, anguish, continuously sitting on a volcano. It can erupt at any moment."[3]

The point is that we do not frantically search for the source but that we get rid of the obstacles. We start to see the unseen signs of a second-choice life, such as not knowing what we really want, an inexplicable emptiness, never-ending fatigue, sacrifice, or a Neverland, and we start taking on the preliminary work.

When we are awake in this process, we effortlessly shift from a second-choice life to a life from the source. We learn to restore contact with the source faster when we lose it. We no longer look for ways; the way will find us. It's not a desired outcome but something that just happens. We take steps on that path, and it happens automatically.

> *Searching for the source distracts us. Life is not a desired outcome, it's something that happens. By opening up to the source, the path will unfold.*
> *When you open yourself up, which path will unfold for you?*

SEEING EVERYTHING FOR THE FIRST TIME IN THE HERE AND NOW

Being present in the here and now can be a route for restoring the connection with our source. By staying grounded and in the here and now, we become more aware of the unique contribution we can make to this world. We then act from the source and don't let our thoughts determine our route.

THE GRINNING MONK

The kite surfer and I had booked a hike through the Markha Valley that departed from Leh, a little village in Ladakh, Northern India. Nine days of hiking and camping in the rugged nature of

continued

the Himalayas with mountain passes of 16,300 feet (4,970 meters) and 17,270 feet (5,265 meters) that we had to cross. I was looking forward to it.

In order to prevent suffering too much from altitude sickness, we decided to acclimatize for a week before the trip started. On the internet, I had found the Mahabodhi International Meditation Center, built by Bhikkhu Sanghasena, a Buddhist monk.[4] In a barren rocky valley at an altitude of 11,480 feet (3,500 meters), he had dug a well, built a house, and planted a vegetable garden. Soon, followers came, and those followers helped him realize his vision for the valley. A temple and a meditation room were built. They built a house for the elderly. After the retirement home, a hospital post followed. After that, a school. He started organizing meditation weeks, and dormitories were opened, which were also accessible to foreign visitors. I found the valley to be the perfect place: a week of meditation and a week of acclimatization at the same time.

We flew to Leh via Delhi and arrived there around noon. The location was sunny, warm, and high. There we were, sitting on a bench in front of the exit of the small airport, gasping for air, directly from our cold flat country to the mighty mountains at 11,480 feet (3,500 meters) altitude. Normally, we would catch a bus, but now we said yes to the first taxi driver who showed up. We really wanted to get to the guesthouse. Getting up to this height in one go was worse than we had imagined.

After signing in and eating some obligatory snacks that the guesthouse owner had made for us, I collapsed on the bed, completely exhausted. The kite surfer lay down next to me. He was having a hard time too, and I felt a little guilty for proposing this trip. But underneath that horrible feeling of wanting to vomit, I also felt butterflies fluttering in my stomach. I sought the kite surfer's hand. We would survive this, and I let myself sink into the battle my body was waging with the altitude.

We stayed in bed all afternoon. The mighty mountains could wait. Every time we fell asleep, we woke up feeling a shortness of breath. We hoped that we would get used to the altitude quickly. We jumped up at about seven o'clock local time because of a loud pounding on the door, in a way as if someone wanted to come through it.

A monk stood behind the door. In broken English, he explained that we had to come along now. The silent retreat started a day earlier than planned, and we were already late for dinner. It was a mystery to us how he had found us, but we packed our bags again in a daze and, a little dizzy from the altitude, we followed the monk outside.

"Wait, the owner of the guesthouse needs to know we're leaving."

"I already told him," the monk said. "Hop in."

He drove an old pickup, and as soon as we sat down, he put his foot on the gas. After leaving the village behind, we came onto a bumpy road. At least that's how it felt because it was already dark outside. There was something surreal about this trip. In a world limited to headlights on a dusty road, we were zooming in a pale red pickup truck driven by a monk in an orange robe and flip-flops through a majestic landscape that was palpable but invisible.

continued

When we arrived at the Mahabodhi Center—according to the monk, because we couldn't see it in the dark—the monk lit a small lantern. He asked us to follow him. I have night blindness, so stumbling along on the kite surfer's arm, I followed the monk along a path that eventually led to a small stone building. Inside, the building was brightly lit with fluorescent lights. It turned out to be the kitchen and canteen. There were bowls of leftover food on tables that were pushed together, and we were heartily welcomed by two people behind the buffet. They filled two plates; they had waited especially for us.

During the meal, the monk informed us about the rules for the week. From the moment we were taken to our sleeping area: complete silence—this applied for the entire week, including not making any eye contact with others. Books, watches, telephones (oh no, my flashlight!), anything that could cause a distraction was confiscated. We would get these items back at the end of the week.

The monk would take the kite surfer to the men's sleeping area, and a young girl from the kitchen came to take me to the women's sleeping area. I had known about the separation in advance, but gosh, no eye contact with others either. As a farewell, the kite surfer and I smiled at each other. This was it for a week, this is what I had wanted.

With another tiny light, the girl took me to some sort of barracks. Here, I shared a space behind one of the doors with another guest who was already sleeping. When the girl with the lamp wanted to leave, I tried to make it clear to her with some gestures that I would like to go to the toilet. She took me by the arm and guided me through narrow corridors and doors as if I were a little child. While the girl stood guard at the toilet door, my pee splashed loudly into the bowl. The butterflies in my stomach had disappeared by now. Okay, I wouldn't be able to find this on my own in the dark, so this had to be it for tonight.

In bed, I tried to surrender to the situation and not panic about the thought that I could be struck by altitude sickness. I had a light headache, but not too bad. I couldn't sleep, and as soon as I dozed off, I felt a shortness of breath, but I had no other symptoms. I tried to figure out where my roommate was to pass the time. She should be somewhere near me, about six feet away. But it was completely silent in the room. I couldn't even hear her breathing.

Finally, out of nowhere, the gong sounded. It was now five o'clock in the morning, the moment the gong would sound. It was still dark, but my roommate turned on the light. Thank goodness. We were not allowed to speak to each other or make eye contact, but I did try to copy her movements. We both got dressed and, armed with a toothbrush and toothpaste, I shuffled behind her to the toilets and sinks.

The route turned out to be much simpler and shorter than I had thought. The narrow hallway ended in a door, and behind that door was a narrow hallway to the toilet and laundry rooms. I couldn't have taken a wrong turn even if I wanted to.

After brushing my teeth, I followed the woman outside. The sun was about to rise, and from the barracks, I followed her to the stairs of the temple and meditation room. From another side, I also saw the men arriving. The stairs looked like they had 4,000 steps. Step by step, I hoisted myself up the stairs, and the

continued

headache started flaring up again. Once at the top, I hung over the railing. The view was phenomenal, and I got a better impression of the facility.

Inside, the room was cozily lit. There were pillows for the participants, and the monk Bhikkhu Sanghasena, who led the retreat, was already sitting on his platform in his orange robe with an alert look and a big grin on his face. I already saw the kite surfer sitting on a pillow. I tried not to look in his direction. He also did his best to avoid eye contact.

There were about a handful of Westerners and a few people from India—from New Delhi, we learned later.

"Ah, you still have both of your legs," Bhikkhu Sanghasena started the day in Indian-English. "Your arms still working, yes? Didn't get ill last night?" His grin became bigger. "No problems now, right?" His eyes started twinkling. "In here and now, never a problem. Future, past—they bring problems, yes!" And so he continued for at least ten minutes.

He talked, he repeated, we were silent. That's how he started every morning before the silent meditation. Every morning, as if he had something new to say. His message about the meaning of living in the here and now seeped into us. There was no escape from it.

Still today, years later, when I think I have a problem, I hear him say it again: "In here and now, never a problem, yes." Then I feel a smile welling up. He's right. If I focus on the here and now—this moment, this second—then, indeed, I don't have a problem. The house is not on fire now, I am not being attacked by a dog, and the debt collector is not knocking on my door. At such a moment, my train of thought comes to a standstill. Then I am back in the temple and see his smiling face. No, I don't really have a problem right now.

A beautiful gift from that monk.

The monk's gift has a broader effect than only staying in the now. Already during that retreat and later while trekking through the mountains, when I stay here and now, I always see the people, animals, plants, and things around me in a new light. At least when I am alert. Being in the now apparently has that side effect. And that side effect teaches me to act according to what the situation demands and not what I think I should do.

Being in the here and now and seeing everything in a new light is a wonderful way for me to restore the connection with my source.

It's a bit like steep wall climbing. I know I want to go up, but I don't focus on the finish line. If I do focus on that, I usually don't make it. While climbing, all my energy and attention are focused on the steps I must take. I always see the gripping points as a new step. Which ones will help me on my way? I act according to what the situation requires and not what I think I should achieve, like the highest point. I also don't look up to see the finish line; I focus completely on the step I am taking.

Being in the here and now and seeing everything in a new light sounds easier than it is. In everyday life, my mind tends to wander off, and every now and then, I am woken up by the memory of the monk's twinkly eyes.

I have experienced that staying in the here and now has brought me clarity and peace, and that's why I practice it regularly. For example, I find it a nice exercise to sit quietly on a chair at home and look at the things around me. In the here and now, without thoughts, I imagine seeing the plants, the cupboard, the rug, the television for the first time. I look at the table, the lamp differently. A feeling of peace comes over me. I feel a sort of solidarity and connection with the source. By doing this exercise regularly, I am able to stay in the here and now and view everything around me in a new light.

Yesterday, tomorrow, the day after tomorrow foresee problems that are often created in our minds. In the here and now, we rarely experience any problems. And by staying in the here and now, we will be able to see the world around us like we're seeing it for the first time.

What do you experience when you sit calmly on a chair and look at the things around you?

STOP LABELING EVERYTHING AND START MAKING REAL CONNECTIONS

Just watch and don't judge. In line with being in the here and now and seeing everything in a new light, it is time to stop labeling things. This allows us to make real connections, not superficial ones tinted by rose-colored glasses, prejudices, or judgments.

On an intellectual level, I understood the concept, but during the second ayahuasca ritual in the Peruvian jungle, I experienced its meaning firsthand.

THE WHITE SNAKE

Just like during the first ritual in which I discovered *love me*, we also lay in the dark maloca during the second ceremony. Because of my experience in the previous ceremony, I was completely relaxed and allowed myself to be carried away by the sound of the drums, the flutes, and the singing of the shamans, interspersed with the night cries from the jungle.

About fifteen minutes after drinking the tea, the images started coming again. I calmly allowed them to come up. This time, I was looking at a white snake coming out of my stomach. The moment I put the label "white" on the snake, a gray spot appeared on the snake, and it retreated back into my stomach. He came out again. I watched as he wriggled out of my stomach.

The label "wriggle" promptly caused a gray spot to appear again, and the snake withdrew. When it appeared for the third time, I carefully avoided "white" and "wriggly," but I was surprised at how long the snake was. Bang! A gray spot for "long." The snake withdrew and came out of my stomach again.

This went on until I stopped labeling, until I stopped judging. I began to connect with the energy of the snake. I refused any thoughts about what the snake looked like, what it was doing, gave it no labels, and simply connected with the snake. The energy

continued

became light and loving, and connecting came naturally, as if the snake and I were one.

The next morning, during the talking-stick ritual, I talked about my experience with the snake. I realized how often I had ideas about myself, how quickly I judged, putting others and, therefore, myself in a box and thus hindering real connections.

Our mind always wants to understand everything, while the energy from the source is just there. But the mind is eager to give meaning to it; unintentionally, it likes to label everything, not realizing that this narrows our view. By putting labels on it, we lose a part of our ability to make a real connection.

The lesson in the Peruvian jungle taught me that the fewer ideas we have about ourselves and others, the more we can let the source flow, the more we can utilize the potential that is at our disposal. The source then effortlessly converts our potential info-focused energy. It encourages action; skills and qualities will manifest themselves.

Now, back to my wall-climbing metaphor. I have dreamed about the view from the top, I trust my agility, and then I set off without any thoughts about how to reach that top. I stay in the here and now. And by not having reviews about the wall's hand holds and not putting labels on them, such as how small, awkwardly turned, or bumpy, I am more likely to see the possibilities that the holds offer. I connect with the holds and move forward.

By refraining from labeling in contact with others, in contact with ourselves, if we let go of all labels, remain silent and grounded, we will always see everything for the first time, and the source unambiguously unfolds our path in front of us.

Our mind unintentionally likes to put labels on everything, but by doing so, we lose a part of our ability to really connect with others and ourselves.

From which labels would you like to free yourself?

LET THE SOURCE WITH YOUR NATURAL QUALITIES DECIDE YOUR PATH

When we are living in connection with our source, we feel more fulfilled, more real. We fulfill our potential. We let ourselves be carried away by the stream of life. With our natural qualities, we add color to the potential that is available to us and make our unique contribution to the world.

Nisargadatta,[5] an Advaita teacher, uses a nice metaphor for this. He explains the all-encompassing energy (in my own words, the source) as an electrical wire with colored and differently shaped lights. We are all connected to the energy that runs through the wire. We are one. It is the life force that makes us shine, that makes us act. Each light in its own way, through its shape, through its color.

If we follow what we were made to do, if we follow the energy in the electric wire, then living in contact with our source could be an effortless process. We just need to let the source flow through us, and our potential provides us with possibilities and direction. Just like the colored lights on the electricity wire.

I sometimes describe the course of the source as water spouting from a fountain. The water just keeps coming. Everything that wants to manifest itself comes from the source. Due to all kinds of events we are unaware of, due to the unseen mechanisms, we close the fountain's opening little by little and place dams in the stream.

And what happens if we put a hand on the opening of the fountain? Then, the water sprays in all directions. Erratic jets of water are created—some hard, some dripping. When we spray teak furniture clean with a garden hose and we squeeze the hose too much, there is such a force on the jet that the teak wood splinters.

The trick is to let the source flow as naturally as possible. If we brick the opening shut, the force within becomes so great that the water seeks refuge elsewhere. A pipe bursts. Or the couplings underground start to leak. In all cases, the water finds a different path, whether we like it or not.

IN A SPANISH CAFÉ

Following the retreat in Andalusia, I booked a plane ticket to Galicia, a province on the northwest tip of Spain. Long coastal walks, visiting *castros* (ruins of the round houses dating from Celtic times), and ending at Santiago de Compostela's pilgrimage site were on my list. Another week of vacation on my own to let the insights I gained at the retreat sink in.

I hopped from town to town with my rental car. According to

the navigation, on the third day, I reached my place to stay near a group of houses, about a mile before the village where I had expected to spend the night. I parked in front of a small café. The village was probably somewhere down the small winding road, but I couldn't see it from my parking spot. The view over the sea, on the other hand, was fantastic. A damp wind blew over the cliff, and the air tasted salty. Now this was living!

The café, a small canteen-like space with a bar, was deserted, but a friendly man wearing a faded brown apron came immediately from behind the counter as I walked farther inside. He smiled broadly and chattered in Spanish, of which I could understand some words. *Habitación*, room, yes, that was me.

"*Reservado la habitación.*" I nodded.

He motioned for me to follow him. My room was on the first floor of the building next door. A blue-and-white-striped tarpaulin hung between the shower and the toilet, there were old-fashioned blankets on the bed, and a wooden kitchen chair stood under a shelf screwed to the wall, but the view was phenomenal. I had booked the room for this reason, and I happily accepted the keys from the man.

"*Lugar, camino*, village, walking," I asked, pointing down in front of the window and hoping my Spanish terms made some sense to him. "Can I *mangiare* there?" I asked, motioning to my mouth with my index finger and thumb. To my shame, I realized that that was Italian for eating, but he understood me.

"*Sí, sí, sí,*" the man said, followed by a few sentences that I didn't understand, but he put his hands on his stomach.

"*Camino minutos?*" I asked.

continued

And again, a flood of words followed, but somewhere in between, I heard *quince minutos*. Only fifteen minutes. That was doable.

After the man had left the room, I kicked off my shoes and put the wooden chair in front of the window. I could sit here for hours. Too bad it was already getting dark, but hey, it was December, so the night fell early.

At about seven o'clock, after a nice warm shower, I got dressed for dinner. I was used to eating alone in a restaurant because of my work, and now I was looking forward to it. I wanted to write about the energy I had felt at the Celtic ruins I had visited that day. So, with my notebook and pen in my bag, I cheerfully went downstairs. When I got outside, it turned out to be pitch dark. No street lights. I hadn't anticipated that. Fifteen minutes of walking with my phone light on in an area I had never been before. I'd rather not. The car, then? A dark, winding road by car? No, that idea didn't appeal to me either. Besides, I was craving some red wine. So, no car. The light was on at the café. Maybe I should try there.

When I stepped inside, the conversations immediately fell silent. All eyes turned to me. Eyes of about eight men. Men at the bar, three men at a table. Men in their fifties and older. Not a woman in sight. Hesitantly, I stood still; maybe I could take the car anyway? But before I could turn around, the café owner shot out from behind the counter and excitedly walked toward me, rattling in Spanish. There were no white-and-burgundy-checkered sheets on the tables, and he had exchanged his pale brown apron for a matching burgundy-red one. I wanted to say that I was going to eat in the village, but he motioned his thumb and index finger to his mouth and made it clear that I could eat here.

"*Sí, mangiare,*" I said uncomfortably.

He grabbed my arm and pointed to the table in the middle. As if it were a five-star restaurant, he pulled out the chair and helped me sit down. The men around me watched my every move. The café owner rambled on until he made a drinking motion.

"*Sí, vino tinto y agua, por favor,*" I said.

"*Excelente, vino tinto,*" he shouted triumphantly through the café.

The men at the bar mumbled agreeingly. Everyone looked happy.

I took my notebook and pen from my bag. The men at the table pointed at it and said something to me. I ignored them.

The café owner put the wine and the water in front of me. "From that gentleman," I understood from his Spanish. A short, chubby man in his fifties at the bar waved cheerfully.

"*No, no, no,*" I responded, annoyed. "On my *cuenta!*"

I regretted that I hadn't turned around immediately at the door. All those men. They just kept looking and commenting every now and then. What did they want from me? In any case, I didn't want anything from them. I looked as mean as possible and decided to focus on my notebook, to pretend they weren't there. But I couldn't write. The fishy incident came back up. Imagine if one of those men wanted to try something. My little voices were looping in my head.

Every time I sipped my wine, the man at the bar started waving happily. I felt the anger build up inside and gave him a cold, haughty look as I refilled my glass from the carafe. He backed off

continued

and said something to the man next to him. I took a deep breath. Ignore them and start writing.

With putting my pen onto the paper, the men indeed disappeared into the background after a while. I wrote about the tingling sensations I had felt in my body at the Celtic ruins. An energetic force was flowing through me, making the sky seem so bright, the grass as alive as I had never seen before. I had been alone there for most of the time, but when other people came, I was fine with that. Feeling connected, feeling completely myself in a group, and what I had learned at the retreat also worked that afternoon. I did not close myself off to the energy field. *I didn't close myself off. Energy field. Energy field.* My pen got stuck on the words "energy field."

The owner brought the food. He placed it gingerly on the table. I looked around in a daze. What had I done with the atmosphere? The happy atmosphere had disappeared. Was that because of me? But I wasn't like that at all. Defensive and haughty didn't suit me. I was curious by nature. I loved chatting with strangers.

The café owner carefully pointed to the two men at the table while stammering something in Spanish. I felt all eyes on me again. Shy now. The men were well-disposed toward me, I felt it in the energy field, and I felt a little ashamed that I had rejected them within five minutes. What was I thinking? Still a bit uneasy, I thanked the men for the food and raised a glass to the man at the bar.

It was as if a fresh breeze had blown through the room. The broad smile returned to the face of the café owner with his burgundy-red apron. The men toasted me, and after I had finished my plate, they sat down at my table. With gestures, a few Spanish words from my side, and a few English words from their side, I understood that they never had visitors coming here. Occasionally, a lone cyclist in the summer, but that wasn't the same. They were proud of their region, their village, and their café, and they were honored to have me. I was their guest. They asked me where I was from. "Ollanda! Johan Cruijff!" Rijkaard. We talked about the Celtic ruins and the ships that used to run aground on their coastline.

I thoroughly enjoyed the evening, the nice men, and the unparalleled hospitality. I was glad that I had cleared the opening of the fountain and that I had been able to let go of my constrictive behavior, my judgments, and my fears. Glad that I had allowed my natural qualities to take in space so that the source could flow.

Manifestation of the source is achieved by allowing the opening of the fountain to spray freely and by touching many hearts with the drops, including our own. When we live in connection with the source, we express with our natural qualities what wants to manifest through us, through the source. We allow to come up what wants to surface. We discover how that works. We discover what makes us want to get up in the morning, what fulfills us, what makes us happy, and how we can help our family and others.

When we don't allow ourselves the time to connect with the energy of the source, when we don't take the time to reflect, we don't see the warning signs (unseen), we outvoice our potential and let our minds determine the route on autopilot, from what we have been taught. At such moments, we listen too much to the people around us, row against the current, and prevent the source from flowing by building dams and closing the fountain's opening.

If we connect to the source and keep the fountain's opening free, we can enjoy our unique contribution to this world. And in the end, that's what it's all about—restoring the connection with the source. Because, as Osho says: "You are not accidental. Existence needs you. Without you something will be missing in existence and nobody can replace it."[6]

The world awaits our own unique contribution. And I have learned that our constructed identity and limiting convictions take us further away from our contribution. We find our place when we let the source and our natural qualities determine the course.

With the source and our natural qualities in control, we can take in our unique space in existence.

How does it feel when you give your natural qualities space and let the source flow?

RELAX WITHIN THE SOURCE

There is nothing better than relaxing in the calm vibrating energy of the source. Just for a moment—no world, no me. Beyond the ideas of "I am this" or "I am that." Just being.

"I am this" already takes shape in our early childhood; the influence of our environment starts when we are put on this earth. Learned behavior arises from that environment. An identity is created from the convictions and skills we develop based on that learned behavior. We all want to be something or someone. The fact that we don't have to be anything doesn't fit in our learned ideas.

We notice that an identity gives us something to hold on

to. Our outside world wants to understand us, and we want to understand ourselves. During introductory rounds at work, you are asked questions such as: Who are you? What moves you? And even though we don't know exactly who we are, we still develop an identity: how we want to see ourselves and how we want others to see us. This is who I am; that is who you are.

Without realizing it, we sometimes strive for ambitions that are too far off from our potential, imposed by our imagined self-image, caused by external pressure. In this way, we want to conform to an image that we think others have of us, formed by impressions that we have interpreted ourselves. And vice versa, we sometimes think that certain goals or activities are not for us due to negative feedback or lack of faith from others. Or we don't explore certain possibilities and qualities because "we just don't do that here" in our family, culture, or social class.

We adopt an identity. This identity no longer comes forth from the source. "I am" becomes "I am this" or "I am that." We give meaning to our thoughts, feelings, and emotions. The identity becomes stronger. In this context, the word "identity" sounds like it has been set in stone, but identity is just as fluid as the potential and the source are. The water pressure changes over time. The arc of the water jet moves along with the sun, the clouds, the wind.

Identity is close to the opening of the source. The more ideas we have about our identity, the more the opening of the fountain becomes bricked up. The fewer ideas about ourselves, the broader we come into our identity, and the more our potential comes into its own through the source. We can then, as it were, reach beyond our (conceived) identity. Inner peace, silence, calmness lie beyond "I am," beyond our limiting convictions and beyond our identity.

AWARENESS UNDERSTANDING
MEDITATION (AUM) MADNESS

During my retreat in Andalusia, I did the OSHO Kundalini Meditation, my first introduction to movement meditations. The shaking and dancing phases of that meditation allowed me to slip into thoughtless silence even faster than during a Zen meditation. At the Midsummer Night Festival that the Humaniversity in Egmond aan Zee organizes annually, various movement meditations were planned, so I really wanted to go there.

At this festival, I participated in the AUM Meditation of Veeresh,[7] a student of Osho and founder of the Humaniversity. AUM stands for Awareness Understanding Meditation. It is a two-and-a-half-hour meditation in which you go through thirteen windows of emotions, such as anger, forgiveness, laughter, crying, madness, joy, silence, and so on.

As newcomers, we were given an explanation in advance about what to expect and what sign we could use to ask for help if the experience became too overwhelming. I felt slightly nervous. The first window was anger. We were supposed to scream, to scream our anger out at whoever was standing in front of us at that moment, someone different every time, for twelve minutes. With my dirty linen syndrome, I wasn't used to screaming, to express my anger. I kept that safely locked in the cellar. In fact, I didn't even know where to look for that anger.

~~~

When the meditation started, all hell broke loose. Astonished, I watched the group of about a hundred people who started shouting at each other with clenched fists and contorted faces. I froze and couldn't move. One of the supervisors grabbed my hand and pulled me into the middle of the group. She shouted at me. There were all kinds of angry people around me. They shouted all kinds of bad things at me: "You treated me badly! I hate you! Why are you standing there with your stupid face? F**k off!" Cautiously, I started shouting back and then louder and louder. I searched for my anger in my cellar. I yelled at my father, my mother, my brother. At the man from the fish packaging company. I let my pent-up anger go. And I had to participate in the ritual to keep the anger high because if I didn't, the anger from the person opposite me would also go away. If you pit anger against anger, it perpetuates itself. I found that a fascinating discovery.

After anger came forgiveness. We had to hug someone and tell them we forgave them. It was cathartic after all the rage. So, windows of emotions came and went until we reached the window of madness. I started out fanatically. Acting crazy, that seemed great to me. But it became so real, so scary. It was almost as if I no longer existed, as if I were being taken over by madness, by an energy of insanity. It was as if one or two tiny Theas seized power and I had no control anymore. They called the shots and terrorized my thoughts and actions. I myself disappeared into the chaos. Panting, I tried to keep myself together until I realized I had nothing to do with that crazy person and that I wasn't that crazy person.

The window of madness had triggered a volcanic eruption. For too long, I had thrown emotions, wishes, and desires into my cellar. Now was the moment when they were given the space to rise from the darkness. The little voices, my thoughts, and emotions seized their opportunity and expressed their displeasure, ranting and screaming.

continued

It had nothing to do with the now anymore. I was taken over by something old. I felt like I was losing all control, and that made me anxious. It all happened in my head, and all kinds of crap came out. Like in a movie, I saw my mouth moving, but this wasn't me.

When I realized that, I became calm. In all that insanity, I found my source, the serene, vibrating energy in which I could rest—a consciousness, a silence, a peaceful feeling. I understood that what we essentially are can't change by whatever experience comes our way; it can't be damaged. From that point, I looked at the people around me and at myself.

This first AUM Meditation taught me that every energy is sustained by a similar amount of that same energy in our environment, whether that be anger, sadness, joy, or madness. With these different energies, people's circles influence each other, not only in such a meditation but everywhere we go. It does not matter whether we experience that energy physically or mentally. For example, if everyone feels unsafe, that environment is unsafe, even if it is only a felt or mentally experienced unsafe.

The experience of no longer existing has kept me busy pondering for a long time. During the AUM Meditation, I experienced that I lost myself during the madness segment, and I extended that to my thoughts about my identity. I wasn't my assumed identity either. But without recognizable stickers or labels on my identity, I felt bare and even frightened. I had nothing to hold on to anymore. I could only let go, carried away by the flow, like water seeking its lowest point. As scary as that was, it was also liberating at the same time.

Better no identity than an invented identity, I thought. In meditation, I found the source, just as I could find the source in a work of art, a sunset, or a walk through the woods in the early morning. In meditation, I found I could rest in the source—the calm, vibrating energy that is always present and where we simply need to be.

Relaxing in the source is a quick way to reconnect with the source. The AUM Meditation was a catalyst for me, but I also discovered other ways that created the same effect. I noticed that by doing something with my full attention, in a way that I get fully absorbed by it, in a way that I strive past my (invented) identity, I also relax in the source. When I have difficulty focusing my attention, I follow the rhythm of my breathing. That helps.

There are many situations in which we can relax in the source—by paying full attention to baking a cake, without any other thoughts, for example, or during a lovely evening of dancing with friends, or by watching the sun set into the sea.

It is also wonderful to relax in the source when we're in contact with other people. Circles of people influence each other; they intertwine. To start, there is a source in each of us, which we all have in common. That source then manifests itself in everyone in their own unique way. We can think of it as a smooth water surface. If we throw several pebbles in it, a wave moment is created from each pebble that hits the surface. Circles in the water are unique; not one circle is the same. The circles the stone makes sometimes collide, sometimes flow into each other. Our unique qualities are diffused by colliding and flowing into each other. But we have to open ourselves up to the source to move beyond those influences.

And when we come back to the source, our space becomes bigger, our impact increases, and our influence on the circles of others becomes more positive without exerting any effort. We simply be and relax in the source, beyond our identity.

The more space we create for our identity, the more we are connected to our source, the more we can relax in our source.

How often do you relax in your source by just being, without additional thoughts?

A SUMMARY OF RECONNECTING

The planting, the restoring the connection with the source, starts with the decision to open ourselves up to the source. Once we have consciously experienced the connection, restoring the connection with the source becomes easier and faster the next time we wander off. Being in the here and now, seeing everything for the first time, refraining from labeling everything, and letting the source walk the path with our natural qualities are tips to help the seeds and the cuttings grow. The goal is to ultimately reap by being able to relax in the source and surrender to the flow called life.

My life changed by restoring the connection with my source. My potential is given space; the path unfolds and is paved more often. And when I stray from it, I quickly restore the connection with the source. And above all, I enjoy the inner peace.

Part III

NEVER GOING
BACK TO A
SECOND-CHOICE LIFE

Chapter 7

KEEPING AN EYE
ON THE SOURCE

I t will take awhile before ingrained patterns can be finally exchanged for new patterns. After divorcing the psychologist, I was determined to go to the ends of the earth to uncover my passions and to be open and speak up in relationships from that point on. But however determined I was, my goal was easier said than done.

Patterns and habits are persistent. The eleventh commandment was persistent. I had to keep reminding myself that I wanted to take this new direction, follow my own path, and fully speak up. I was so used to keeping my thoughts to myself. And old patterns keep popping up. Until we have firmly established the new pattern, we're extra vulnerable to relapse into our old pattern.

Our brain needs time to make new connections and paths and to leave the old ones for what they are. That's how it works biologically. The old familiar neurological network is strong. The new neurological network, our newly formed pattern, is still vulnerable. Therefore, our brain prefers to stick to the old unless it becomes convinced that the new path provides it with advantages. And our brain is not easily persuaded in doing so, not even when we have reconnected with our source. Living effortlessly certainly feels uncomfortable at first. From our childhood onward, we are trained to set a goal and work toward it. We often don't know what to do with all that effortlessness. We were raised with the idea that we must persevere and, if necessary, row against the current to achieve the results that are worth pursuing in the eyes of those around us.

In my brain, the eleventh commandment was a deeply ingrained path, a familiar route I had often taken on autopilot, even before I knew it. In such moments, I had to retrace my steps to follow my new path. I needed more time to respond, and sometimes that felt like a secondary response.

THE ORGANIZATIONAL RAKE

In my work, I once developed a new organizational chart with a client's management team different from a traditional hierarchical rake system. This new system consisted of circles with equal teams that shared a collaborative agenda and were facilitated by the management board. Inspired by the vision of Ricardo Semler, the chart had room for cross-team projects in which anyone with the right motivation could participate.

With great enthusiasm, we reorganized and were invited to talk about it at a meeting with executives and CEOs. Although the reorganization was inspiring, it was also hard work. Everyone had to get used to the new system, both employees and managers. We received not only praise but also criticism. After the setup, my project ended, a board member and a team leader resigned, and two circles merged. To my dismay, even before the new organization and the new pattern had taken hold, the organization reverted back to the hierarchical rake, which was less inspiring but much more familiar.

I was quite distraught that this happened. It almost hurt me physically. Should I have developed the model better? Why had management given up so quickly? When the CEO delivered the news, it was difficult for me not to judge him. All that effort and money for nothing. I felt guilty for the team members who had started the idea with such inspiration.

The CEO listed valid arguments for his decision. Perhaps the new organizational model had been too good to be true, I thought. And I simply couldn't force anyone to follow my path. I heard the monk Sanghasena laughing in my head: *So, you have a problem now?* No, I didn't. And worrying about the past and future is pointless. I stopped worrying.

It is one of the most difficult assignments we can give ourselves: to do things differently from now on. But through trial and error, I have learned that if we can maintain the new pattern for a while, it will eventually become just as effortless as the old pattern.

Just like our brains, we also unconsciously maintain old patterns with our bodies. Our body stores all kinds of memories.

When we've experienced a situation that we liked or didn't like, our body stores that energy, that feeling, in our cells.

I once fell off a ladder, and I still tremble when climbing one. This is also how it works with emotional periods that we go through. Tension, fear, uncertainty—the emotions store themselves in our bodies.

Our cells may have retained information that we can no longer remember, both good and not-so-good memories. As a result, we are unknowingly controlled by our bodies that make decisions or respond in ways we don't mean to.

THAT POOR BUTCHER

After the fishy incident, I became a shopgirl at the butchery. The butcher was a big, friendly man, caring and sociable. He taught me how to make the tastiest steak tartare. I was allowed to operate the mincer by myself, and I turned out to be quite handy with the cutting machine.

On Saturdays, there were usually three of us in the shop—the butcher, the permanent shop assistant, and me. The atmosphere was pleasant, and the variety of cutting meats, mincing, and serving customers made the job easy to continue. The only problem was my height. I had trouble removing the meat from the front of the display case.

Once, an old lady with a glittery handbag wanted three schnitzels. I managed to get out two of the three. The third had slumped against the window of the display case. With my hips on the counter, my arm stretched out as far as possible, and my legs dangling, I tried to reach that last schnitzel. While I was hanging with my head in the display case, the butcher leaned forward and took the schnitzel. A sudden shock went through my body. Back on my feet, I furiously pushed him aside.

"Hey, let me help you with that schnitzel," the butcher responded angrily.

My cheeks flushed, as I was mortified about my response.

"The little lady seems actually quite capable of helping herself," the glitter-bag lady grumbled at the butcher. "Good girl, don't let them walk all over you. Too often, men seem to think that we women are lost without them," she said indignantly.

Bewildered, I looked over the counter at the old lady. She really seemed to mean it. She looked belligerently at the butcher.

The butcher was stumped for words, just like I was.

Uncomfortably, he stood there with the schnitzel in his hand. "That, eh, that is not what I meant. I just wanted to help," he stumbled to the lady. For a second, I thought he wanted to put the schnitzel back, but thankfully, he put it on the scale. "Apologies," he said to me, and quickly, he disappeared to the back of the store.

That afternoon, I didn't understand why I had responded so intensely. But when I lay awake at night, I understood that he had come too close to me. Even though I knew I had nothing to fear from this man, my body responded with an intense shock.

My body had been reminded of the fishy incident. That poor butcher.

Living according to the source remains an ongoing process because once we've reconnected with our source, it doesn't mean that from that moment on, we have forever learned to live according to the source. As I mentioned earlier, life seems designed to pull us back into a second-choice life, so even though we have reconnected with our source, there will still be times that we stray again.

Particularly in the initial period, when we have not yet developed new patterns, when our old patterns emerge, when our environment still responds uncomfortably to our new course, when our body unconsciously sends us in the same old direction, we can really use some support.

TOOLS TO HELP YOU STAY ON YOUR PATH

To minimize the chance of straying and to stay as close to the source as possible, I have included some tools in this chapter to help you stay on your course. Particularly in the initial period, I found the following tools to be quite useful. In addition, I have had a lot of fun with them and still use them occasionally.

THE CIRCLE: VISUALIZATION–
LEARNING–INSPIRING

Visualization is a fascinating tool. Visualization helps us to learn new actions. When we start taking driving lessons, we have to perform all kinds of actions at the same time: looking, braking, accelerating, shifting gears. It has been scientifically proven that if we practice actions in our heads through visualization, our brain already paves a path with connections so that those actions that still have to come into practice become easier. This concept applies to everything we do. Conducting, swimming, building, it doesn't matter what it is. A dry run in our head helps.

While writing this book, I visualized the process: I saw myself writing. Felt the joy of it. When I felt resistance, I saw myself asking where that resistance was coming from. I practiced moving past that resistance.

That resistance usually consisted of a conviction that no longer served me or an excuse, because I felt insecure or thought I couldn't do it. With the visualization, I bypassed my tiny Theas and maintained my connection to the source. I saw myself writing, and I felt happy. My source hadn't sent me on this path for nothing—dreaming and trusting.

By combining visualization with learning and inspiration, a powerful circle is created.

Learning from others. We can take inspiration from the people we admire, who may already be well-versed in a subject that interests us. I like to read books and stories from authors I admire. We can also take lessons to increase certain skills. Once a month, I meet up with former fellow students from the Writers' School. In addition to our personal experiences, we talk about writing experiences, learn from each other, and inspire each other.

Part of learning is also telling others about our progress. This can be done in a conversation but also through text message or chat—it doesn't matter. It's about showing ourselves. This teaches us to express ourselves, to share our dreams and thus bring them into the world. When we talk about our journey out loud, we conquer our environment instead of the other way around. We automatically surround ourselves more often with people who support us, encourage us, or are like-minded. We learn to take in the space we need so that we dream and we're not being dreamed about too often.

MY NEIGHBOR AND BLUE LARKSPUR

During my Writers' School period, I had my neighbor at the time read all my writing. Her name is Carry, just like my soul sister but with a "y." She is a flamboyant woman, the mother of the neighborhood, and very well-read.

In addition to correcting punctuation and spelling errors in my texts, she provided me with specific feedback. "You did a great job, you showed the deceased through the eyes of the young woman," she said, for example. Or, with triumphant twinkly eyes: "No, no, no, that's not how it works in real life, little lady. You really can't describe it that way!" And then I had no other option than to rewrite the piece because, most of the time, she was right.

I once described the individual flowers of the blue larkspur—my favorite flowers—as "delicate ballerinas with wide-hooped skirts." From that moment on, she could never look at a blue larkspur the same again. I loved that.

The texts we read together led to great conversations. She

talked about her life, her mother who had the courage to immi-
grate to Canada alone, and her relationship with her brother and
her kids. I told her about my life, about the choices I had made. I
learned from her, and she learned from me.

By sharing my writing every week, she joined me in my dream
of becoming a writer. She followed my progress closely and took
my writing seriously. That has helped and strengthened me to per-
manently create space for writing in my busy schedule.

With what we have learned, we can **inspire** others. I thought it
was scary to consciously put on the gown of inspiration. Who am
I to imagine that I can inspire others, I asked myself. But I learned
that by sharing practical knowledge, insights, or amazement, I got
used to my own personal leadership.

After retreats, I made my friends and neighbors part of the
meditations I had done or insights I'd had. At home, for example,
I put on the CD of the OSHO Kundalini Meditation, turned the
volume up to 10, and together with my friends and the kite surfer,
we were shaking and dancing in the living room. That kind of
sharing felt natural; it didn't feel inspiring, but it was.

I started taking on the role of inspirer more consciously when
I tried out, with a group of women, a program I had put together
based on exercises and insights I'd had, which I called the Switch
program. With Switch, I wanted to inspire women to discover
their own natural qualities and sources. I deliberately put on the
inspiration gown, though still hesitant. And that was noticeable.
I had trouble running the program in a structured manner, and I

didn't provide enough insight into the motivations and direction it had brought me. I still held on to a few limiting convictions (who did I think I was?) that blocked the flow of my source. Even so, these were nice meetings. I got a little taste of what it was like to be an inspiration. I have now also started getting used to my personal leadership in this area, something I have done many times before in my work.

After the Switch program, I started working on an adventure novel. I had already plotted the entire storyline when I began to feel a strong need to write the book you are reading now. It felt as if an invisible hand was pushing me toward that direction while my limiting convictions were still sputtering. I cleared those convictions away. The adventure novel would just have to wait. Apparently, it was time to take a new step. Now, I consider it an honor if I manage to inspire other people.

～～～

If we pay close attention, we notice that we inspire and teach others more often than we initially thought. By doing this consciously, we not only help others but also ourselves. The best students have students of their own. It's wonderful when we can transcend ourselves. Everyone has their own view of the world and has been through difficulties, and when we share those, we help others struggling with similar issues, sometimes even without knowing it. With our information, we can accelerate the path of others, teaching them the skills they need faster than if that information had not been there. We learn and then we inspire.

In short, the powerful circle of visualization—learning—inspiring consists of:

1. Visualization: dream and envision yourself manifesting your potential

2. Learn from others and teach others

3. Inspire by sharing

Check whether you give your natural qualities enough space. When learning and inspiring, try to avoid labeling, and instead view everything as if you are seeing it for the first time as much as possible.

~~~~

To keep an eye on the source and not fall back into old patterns, I kept a simple matrix to monitor my actions (see table 7.1). I evaluated what I did over the past week to stay close to my source or what kept me from it, as well as how I felt about the past week.

Every week, I put a check mark or a cross beside visualization, learning, and inspiring.

And if I do not put a check mark beside one of the three, no worries, every week there's a new opportunity. It's about awareness; there is no final exam. It's a tool to stay connected to the source.

Example matrix

WEEK	1	2	3	4	5	6	7	8	9
Visualization	√	√	√	√	√	√	√	√	√
Learning	√	X	√	√	√	√	X	√	√
Inspiring	X	√	X	√	X	X	X	√	√

Table 7.1

THE SCRIPT OF THE SOURCE

The script of the source is applicable to all areas of life: relation-ships, work, family, spare time. My example is about my job.

In the years after divorcing the psychologist, I was completely focused on my child, on my search for the source, and on changing my way of dealing with relationships. Everything seemed to be running smoothly at work, but it cost me more and more energy, and I felt restless. The second-choice alarm bells were going off. At the same time, I felt resentment. I had made progress in one area, but had I taken steps back in another?

At work, I saw myself as a successful professional; that is how many people in my environment and at work saw me too. Still, something kept gnawing, and now I recognized that feeling: I had drifted into a second-choice life at work. What that second choice exactly was or what had caused it, I couldn't exactly pinpoint. Was this caused by my own idea of my identity, my convictions, my behavior, the environment, or a combination of factors? Where did I feel stuck? Where had I built the most dams? To find out, I drew the following concentric circles.

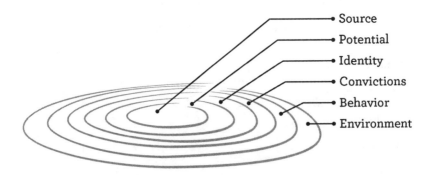

Rings and New Words: Bringing the Script of the Source in Four Steps into Practice

I imagined the source letting energy flow from the middle of the circle into the other rings.

The potential is closest to the source. This ring is where our unique contribution lies. We give direction by means of our natural qualities to that which wants to manifest itself through the source. The identity picks up on that, gives it meaning, and implements the convictions. Convictions lead to behavior, and we express that in our environment. Therefore, the environment is the outer ring, which is farthest away from the source.

I looked at the picture and wondered in which ring I had built the dams that kept me from connecting with my source in my work situation. I turned it into a fill-in-the-blank exercise. (Feel free to join in if you like, choosing your work, family life, sports life, or another area of life.)

Step 1: Writing Down the Status Quo

In my work, I assigned myself the following **identity**:

> Stable—problem solver—trustworthy—diplomat/
> connector—knowing what is going on—knowing what
> has to be done.

This identity that I assigned myself partly arose from my potential. For example, I had checked off the quality of the connector, and from that quality, I developed the self-image that I can bring different parties together. But a large part of that assumed identity was based on how people see me.

Clients and colleagues seek me out when a department or business unit needs to be reorganized or needs to get better results. Clients and colleagues see me as a problem solver. They rely on my leadership to bring a business unit or department (back) to a successful level, together with the employees. I am also deployed to finalize deals, clear the air, or enter into relationships with other companies as a diplomat and a connector. In that role, people find me trustworthy.

Accustomed to the way people approach me and appeal to my talents, I unconsciously identified myself with certain functions and roles and accepted them as a part of my identity.

The list of the ring of **convictions** looks as follows:

Second in command—behind the scenes—
multitalented—workhorse—modest—ethical/
integrity—responsible—quickly seeing through
things—courageous/daring.

I noticed I had written down different terms for the same thing: second in command, behind the scenes, modest. I left them as nuances for a complete picture. I frowned when I saw the word workhorse. I realized then that I was a hard worker without asking myself whether I thought it was worth the energy. It was my conviction that I had to take on the work with responsibility and be courageous and daring in it.

Behavior: What did I bring into the world in my work? I

thought about the feedback I received. Somehow, I felt some resistance to writing down words that characterize my behavior. It's as if I cast myself in stone with those words. But I wrote down what came to mind anyway. This was the list:

> Goal/result-oriented—action-oriented—
> problem-solving—not always going for the best solution,
> but for support—focused on the leader/client—
> in the background—serving.

If this was my behavior, what would my work **environment** look like? I wrote down the following:

> Requesters—support seekers—political administrators—
> lonely leaders—problem solver—fixing odd jobs—emptying
> and cleaning the metaphorical cesspool.

When describing my environment, I shifted to my role in the environment. Problem solver, handyman, someone who empties and cleans the cesspool—these were the descriptions assigned to me by those around me. I left them because the role I gave myself was significant enough to consider what kind of people or companies I attracted and in what role I thought I would be of value to those around me. Identity and convictions led to the behavior.

When I read back what I had written down in the rings about my work situation, I felt myself tense up. Did I really see myself that way? Gone was my idea of a successful self-employed professional. Unmistakably second choice.

I found my second-in-command idea the most baffling. In my circle of friends, I am not necessarily the pacesetter, but in a social environment, I never thought of myself in terms of first or second in command. Why did I do that in my work? In the end, I was the one who had written that down.

Not going for the best solution but for support naturally fit in perfectly with my role as a connector and diplomat. Compromising. Still, it didn't feel good. It annoyed me even. I looked like a political party instead of a decisive leader.

Okay, there were also some beautiful things in the list, recognizable things, but it struck me that I had put down workhorse when it came to convictions. Workhorse. I envisioned tourists riding on donkeys, and I was the donkey with an overweight tourist on my back. I imagined myself standing exhausted in the meadow after a long working day, enjoying the fresh green grass.

And gosh, I hadn't described my environment as very inspiring. Of course, in my work I was asked to solve problems, empty and clean the cesspool, but that didn't necessarily have to go hand in hand with people asking for help and seeking support. My image was clear; I had correctly sensed the gnawing at my soul.

Step 2: Crossing Out and Adding New Words
That Feel More Appropriate (Also Check Your
List of Natural Qualities)

I went back to the ring of **identity**. The words problem solver didn't sit right with me. Yes, I was often hired to solve problems, and in my private environment, people also always knew how to find me, but I thought about the lesson the snake had taught me. Wasn't it just a label I had given myself?

Problem solver sounded cool, but it felt like a label, a tag that I didn't want to wear. *Before I knew it, as a problem solver, I was not really connected or being dreamed. I outsource something essential when I see myself as a problem solver. It is an invitation to all people to call for my help, and then what remains for myself?* I decided that problems didn't exist, only situations. I said goodbye to the identity of the problem solver and crossed out the word.

What I missed in my identity was creating and inspiring. I loved to paint and draw, made a film about energetic power spots, and wrote stories. And in my list of natural qualities stood imagination; the other side of fantasy is manifesting through imagination, something that is fitting for inspirers. The identity that felt closer to my source was one of inspirer, who creates and manifests what arises from the source and is provided by the potential. A creator. The words connector and trustworthy felt good. I left those.

In the ring of **convictions** I changed second in command into leader/inspirer. With my new identity, I had to *love me*. Behind the scenes and modest, I changed into: getting things done through collaboration, networking, and sharing. I added: from vision to realization, doing what you want to do. I left responsible and courageous/daring. Those felt good.

At first, I changed workhorse into parade horse. But I crossed that one off quickly. I didn't want to be anyone's horse. If I wanted to be a horse, then I'd be a wild horse.

In the ring of **behavior**, I left action-oriented. I crossed off problem-solving. I wanted to get the best out of people. Go for the best solution, the best result. Not seeing problems but situations. From being dreamed, I shifted to dreaming.

I wanted to see boundaries as signposts to push those boundaries and embrace adventure. "Be realistic, plan for a miracle" is one of my favorite quotes by Osho. Imagining and realizing a vision—that's what I wanted for myself and for others. Sharing and trusting. It made me happy. I noticed that the additions I had written down fitted seamlessly with my natural qualities.

It was going well and my **environment** felt brand new. I wrote down daredevils, pioneers, trendsetters, adventurers, builders, sharers. Hallelujah, what a different list than the one I had written down during the scan of my current situation. I wondered: would I also be able to get projects in such an environment?

When I read back my adjustments, I felt happy and giggly. I shyly said yes to being an inspirer and creator. Although they felt true, these two words were outside my comfort zone. I would desperately need the courage that I had written down under my convictions.

I noticed that it felt liberating to cross out the words that I didn't want to be anymore. I was determined to abandon those words (patterns) and replace them with new ones.

Step 3: Reflection—Meditate for a Few Minutes before You Start

After staring into the void for a few minutes, I thought back to the start of my work as an entrepreneur. My motivation then was to help companies and organizations move forward. That included solving problems, but over the years, I had more or less made that a goal. By doing so, I had drifted off my path. I had become trapped in my identity and convictions. *Second in command*—what was I thinking? And *a workhorse*—that stemmed from my childhood.

But now there were the new words: inspirer and creator. I thought of Bhikkhu Sanghasena. He had turned a barren rocky valley at an altitude of 11,480 feet (3,500 meters) into an oasis containing a temple, retirement home, hospital, and school.

When I expressed my admiration about this after the silent retreat, he shook his head: "That's not what it's about. The most important thing is that all those people who visit the center, who helped build it, feel a spark of inspiration. They have seen how you can mean something to others together, what you can achieve together." And: "Those people go back to their family, go back to the country they came from. But that spark and this valley will stay with them forever."

Then I remembered why I started doing this work. For me, organizations and companies have a fundamental place in society. People and companies can make a difference and make the world a better place. Helping companies and (individual) employees to make an impact, helping them to stay true to themselves, feels more like my path. Making a profit is healthy, it makes development possible, but making a profit as the only goal to get up for in the morning is not me. I have always felt that way.

And if employees are in the right place, if they know what they are specifically contributing to, they can fly. I had experienced that so many times. An improvement in performance and profitability followed automatically.

I chuckled. All things considered, my motivations at work were still the same, except that I had fallen asleep somewhere on the way and handed over the wheel to those around me (CEOs, shareholders, colleagues). I let myself be labeled and had labeled myself. I had considered the ideas about my identity and convictions to be true. From an essential human being, I had become a doer, in the words of Osho.

Step 4: Practicing

I immediately put into practice the renewed vision that I had gained by filling in the rings. I shifted my focus from solving problems to helping people realize their full potential and, therefore, make the team or business unit function better. And being second in command—no, I didn't do that anymore.

The interesting thing was that I quickly discovered that I didn't have to get rid of my work environment. Some clients may have left, but most people and clients responded well to my new path. I addressed other aspects of my clients.

For me, it was an eye-opening experience, and at the same time, it made a lot of sense. People respond to each other. People look for confirmation from each other. I myself do that, and others do that too. The moment I start walking a new path, it provides space for others to show other sides of themselves. So, I didn't lose any clients, but my projects became different, more focused on development and innovation instead of solving problems and emptying the cesspool.

My clients did have to get used to my new approach. I insisted on being given enough space to do whatever I thought was necessary. I expected a commitment in advance to work more organically with a team, which required trust because the result would only become visible after about six months but would last longer. At first, I found it scary, and I wondered whether my new approach would turn out well. It turned out to be an unnecessary fear. I became more authentic in my leadership, and my new course of action turned out more positively than I could have imagined. From a second-choice work life, I had restored the connection with my source again.

I called the picture with the fill-in-the-blanks exercise the script of the source. The script made it clear to me where I had stuck the yellow Post-it labels and where I had allowed others to put them. This insight allowed me to shake them off, allowing the source to flow again the way it was meant to flow.

A CONTRACT WITH YOURSELF

A contract with yourself is a wonderful tool for living from your source. A sample contract is included at the back of this book. We write down what we are working on in the contract, but a timetable is not necessarily included. If we feel that we want to finish something in two months, for example, that is, of course, allowed, but think back to my wall-climbing example. You don't know in advance which grips you will use and how long it will take you. The result can't always be determined in advance. The result may look different than we first envisioned. It is about acting in connection with the source. We take steps that the situation requires at that moment.

BUSY WITH WORK

During one of the monthly meetings with former fellow students of the Writers' School, I discussed the slump I was in. Writing wasn't going well for a while, and I was barely making any progress.

"I'm too busy with work," I complained.

"Then work less."

"I have a contract, it's impossible," I countered.

"Ah," one of my former fellow students said, "that is the essence for you. Make a contract with yourself, then you have to. Then you write wonderfully. Nothing can come in between—no work, no family-related things."

We laughed about it, but there was some truth to it. Why hadn't I made a contract with myself? Earlier, a woman had said to me: "Write your book like you're running your business. Make a plan and stick to it. Plan it like you plan your work."

At that moment, that advice didn't land. Writing was something creative, it had nothing to do with a business environment. But when my former fellow student said: "Make a contract with yourself," that advice did resonate with me.

The contract is meant to stay awake, live in connection with your source, and not drift off your path. Think up consequences for when you don't stick to the contract or when you do. Make this part of the contract.

It works better to include a horror image for some people: "If I don't stick to the contract, I will place a stool in the middle of the market square and pretend I am a witch." It can be less daring, as long as it is something you really don't like.

For me, rewards work better than punishments. Like a dog, I learn faster with cookies as a reward. Before finishing this book, I promised myself a ticket to Oregon to visit my soul sister, whom I hadn't seen in several years except via Zoom. It doesn't matter what we choose, as long as it has an impact on us.

Then, check what is written in the contract once a month or after six months. Are you still on your way to connecting with your source?

If you have made a contract, commit to it.

Our soul doesn't take no for an answer. Life will talk back, and the lessons will become harder. Laugh about the slip-ups along the way. It's okay. It's trial and error. Recently, I saw a guest on a Tony Robbins motivational talk show who said: "Trust your get-up." I liked that: trust that you can get up if you fall. We are all more resilient than we think.

We are worthy of a life in connection with our source.

THE FAN CLUB

I have borrowed the fan club concept from Willem de Ridder. Following his book *Spiegelogie (Guide to Mirrorology)*,[1] fan club meetings were organized throughout the Netherlands. In such a fan club, you are treated as a star, and in turn, you are a devoted fan of the others in the group. Everyone supports each other unconditionally, a club of dedicated fans of each other.

The meeting with my former fellow students works the same way as a fan club. They keep me going, they support me, and I have fun with them. Our paths don't have to be the same; everyone follows their own path, but the obstacles we encounter along the way, the encouragement, work the same for everyone.

With a number of people in your environment, you may already have your own fan club. You can always start one yourself. But you are also welcome to join a fan club of readers of this book; please email your personal details to fanclub@thearotteveel.com.

However we do it—online, physically, or via a combination of the two—a fan club keeps us on our toes. We create an environment that supports and encourages us when things sometimes are not going well. Asking for help is difficult. But not in our fan club. Saying your dream out loud is scary. But not in our fan club. It is difficult to admit that things are not going well. But not in our fan club.

In a fan club, we influence, inspire, and help each other. In a fan club, we learn that we get ahead when we show ourselves. We surround ourselves with people who are on their way and who are really going for it. A fan club helps us to stay connected to the source. The fans know that the world is waiting for our unique contribution.

Chapter 8

ACCEPT THE INVITATION FROM YOUR SOURCE

The way back to the source is a beautiful journey that has brought me much joy. Without the boulders and rocks in my stream, I wouldn't even have started. It took a crisis, a divorce while I had a young child, for me to realize that I was slowly losing my soul. The more I persisted in a second-choice life, the harder the lessons became, and the louder life started talking back at me.

Once I started recognizing the warning signs (unseen), there was no way back. I acknowledged with astonishment what I had told myself: *It is better to remain silent. I have to be the breadwinner, otherwise things will go wrong. My help is needed. A good mum doesn't divorce. I said I would do it, so I have to do it. This is simply expected of me.* These are all arguments of my mind, imposed by my assumed identity and limiting beliefs inspired by my environment. These arguments were blocking my source.

From all the teachers in my life, from Mrs. Heijdenrijk in primary school to the shamans in Pucallpa, the monk Sanghasena in Ladakh, and all the Advaita teachers and other teachers I have visited, I have learned that to restore the connection with the source, I must see myself completely. *Love me.* With *love me* and my potential, I crossed the threshold on the way to a life in connection with the source. I got to know my regular traveling companions: the tiny Theas, my little voices. I got to know them, to love them, and to bypass them.

I replaced hope with dreaming and trusting. I determinedly followed the-force-that-knows-the-way. Sometimes everything went smoothly and I celebrated my success, and other times I found myself in a rut. But there is nothing wrong with being in a rut. A rut provides beautiful insights. Don't believe people who say everything is always going smoothly for them.

An old story I heard during a retreat was very helpful to me: Once upon a time, there was a woman who had lost her child. The woman was desperate with grief and visited a monk, asking him to bring her child back to life. The monk answered: "I will bring her back to life if you find a house in this village that does not bear a cross of its own." The hopeful woman went to all the houses in the village. Everywhere she knocked on the door, people who once had lost a loved one answered. No matter how difficult her loss was, the woman understood what the monk had meant.

~~~

We gain insights on the way back to the source. We see a glimpse of the source. We are on our way, but our path has potholes. We may encounter joy and happiness but also disappointment, sadness, and despair. Still, it is a beautiful road, one that brings us closer to ourselves, on which we can live our full potential.

For me, the source is an unimaginable force that permeates everything. Everything has its own quality. Every time I think of that, I stand on the mountain in Ladakh, where the sunrise was poured into my soul. And in that grandeur, I could only be silent.

There are no words for the amazement we have about the miracle of creation; talking about it is only to be silent. The tiny Theas are trying to find their space within it. Those voices on the left shoulder and voices on the right shoulder are trying to maintain themselves within it. Dualism is part of being human. Dark and light influence each other. Both are necessary. There is no right or wrong.

For me, restoring my connection with the source has been an adventure that took years. I laughed, I cried, I became my own friend. Sometimes I got stuck, sometimes I relapsed, but I always bounced back. And if I stray now, I find my way back to the source more quickly. Along the way, it became clear to me that life is waiting for us. Always. It awaits our unique contribution to the world. Without us, something is missing. There is a loss.

So, even if we have wandered off a hundred times, we can reconnect at any time. Because everything that happens in our lives—boulders and rocks—is an invitation to return to the source.

ACKNOWLEDGMENTS

L oved ones, family, friends, colleagues, neighbors, fellow students, teachers, monks, shamans, spontaneous encounters, unknown passersby, fellow travelers—there are many people who have contributed to my life and therefore contributed to the creation of this book. I thank you all!

A special acknowledgment to Harry, my dear partner. Our wonderful conversations, your unwavering support, and your unconditional encouragement were invaluable to this book. And also to Enno, my beautiful son. I benefited so much from our tireless brainstorming during our dinners, from your infectious fire to go for it, and from your input in the design.

I am extremely happy for all my good friends, family, and former neighbor; thank you so much for your support, humor, and for believing in me.

Many thanks to my writing coach, Jeanet van Omme. There was that spark between us from the very first moment we met. With the help of your critical but always positive feedback, this book managed to wedge itself up like a dandelion in the pavement so the radiant wreath of flowers could turn toward the sun.

Kudos to you: Marcelle, Daphne, Esther, Thomas, Carry, Enno, and Harry. Your feedback after reading the manuscript not only made the book better but also strengthened me to go forward with the publication process.

Louise Koopman, thank you for the great editing; it has made this a better book. And I enjoyed our "language" conversations, Jeanine Tanis. You were more than entrusted with preparing it for printing. Nathalie from Villa Grafica, your enthusiasm and imagination have ensured that this book has been designed in a way that suits me and the book itself. Marjolein from Moens Photography, with your cheerful and quick response, the cover photo has the exact energy I wanted from it.

Thank you, Laura Woolthuis of Sesquipedalious, for the translation from Dutch to English, and Carrie Teerman for reviewing the initial English transcript. And my enormous thanks to the fantastic Greenleaf Team, who handled the entire publishing process with great enthusiasm and craftsmanship.

And a special word of thanks to you, dear reader of this book, for allowing me to cross your path with this book.

Appendix A

BLANK CHART AND LIST WITH NATURAL QUALITIES

CARE FOR A LITTLE EXERCISE?

Fill in the chart for yourself. Write down three to five qualities per quadrant. A quality may appear in multiple quadrants. Start at quadrant 1 and work clockwise to quadrant 4.

My Toolbox with Natural Qualities

1. QUALITIES I LIKE OF MYSELF OR THAT MAKE ME HAPPY	2. QUALITIES I DON'T LIKE, THAT I PREFER TO IGNORE
1.	1.
2.	2.
3.	3.
4.	4.
5.	5.
4. QUALITIES THAT OTHERS ADMIRE IN ME	**3. QUALITIES THAT OTHERS ACCUSE ME OF HAVING**
1.	1.
2.	2.
3.	3.
4.	4.
5.	5.

Good and bad qualities don't exist. Each characteristic has its own quality and can be experienced in different ways by yourself or others. For example, adventurousness can be seen as restlessness. And restlessness can be appreciated because this quality encourages action; you are not satisfied with the situation as it is.

Here you can find a list of qualities and how they can be experienced. There are many more qualities; this list is intended to help you get started.

QUALITY	HOW IT MIGHT BE EXPERIENCED
Adventurous	Loose, unclear, restless
Courageous/daring	Overconfident, risky, daredevil
Enterprising	Dominant, takes control, opportunistic
Risk-averse	Cautious, well-informed
Control freak	Stays on course
Connector	Ignores individual needs, tends toward compromising
Mediator	Only concerned about supporting and doesn't always go for the best solution
Collaborator	Team player, ignores individual qualities, doesn't stand up for themselves
Loner	Finds their own way and lives independently
Impersonal	Considers everything to be business, stress-resistant
Result-oriented	No attention for the atmosphere, the goal justifies the means
Reliable	Goody two-shoes, has difficulty going back on decisions
Responsible	Haughty, serious, earnest
Careless	Experimental, often heroic and steps into the breach
Impulsive	Spontaneous and enthusiastic, knows how to make quick decisions

QUALITY	HOW IT MIGHT BE EXPERIENCED
Fickle	Agile, lively
Optimistic	Carefree, insufficiently assesses risk, reckless, guileless
Cheerful	Easy, light, superficial
Sensitive	Empathetic, sentimental, tenderhearted
Meek	Others go first, (too) tolerant
Insensitive	Not easily disturbed, unperturbed and calm
Intimidating	Powerful personality, gets things done
True to yourself	Self-centered, sometimes harsh in the eyes of others
Combative	Fanatic, intolerant
Temperamental	Boisterous, wild, wears their heart on their sleeve
Good listener	Opinionless, suppresses their own expression
Caring	No attention to one's own needs, doesn't take in their own space
Pessimistic	Negative, an eye for risks
Perfectionist	Only concerned with details, overprotective, needs time to achieve a goal
Structured	Inflexible, difficulty with improvising
Creative	Vague, chaotic
Imaginative	Resourceful, sometimes not very realistic
Solution-oriented	Takes not enough time for the process, (too) action-oriented
Leader	Overestimates themselves, bossy, intimidating
Resilient	Flexible, adapts too much, follower
Resolute	Dogged, decisive
Inspiring	Not a good listener, (too) exuberant
Open-minded	Impressionable, susceptible to the opinions of others

EXAMPLE OF A CONTRACT WITH YOURSELF

A contract with yourself is a tool to stay connected to your source.

- √ Write down the things that you want to work on. Don't make the steps too big. Small steps eventually lead to big changes.

- √ Choose three dates on which you evaluate your actions. Stay positive while doing so and be kind to yourself.

- √ Think of a consequence when you do or don't follow through with your intention. For some, it works better to think of something you really don't like, a negative consequence when they don't stick to their contract. For others, a reward works better. Find out what motivates you the most.

- √ See whether you want to stick to your contract after six months or whether you have gained new insights that you want to work with.

CONTRACT WITH MYSELF

The next six months, I will be working on:

(for example, something practical, writing a book, getting in shape, but it can also be less practical, like showing more of myself at work, speaking up for what is important to me in my relationship, etc.)

Therefore, it is necessary that I:

(for example, for writing a book: that I write at least an hour a day; for speaking up about what is important to me in my relationship: that I ask myself every night before going to bed if I said what I wanted to say and that I make time every week to talk to my partner about it)

On the following dates, I will evaluate the progress of this contract:

1.

2.

3.

These dates are noted in my planner.

If I don't stick to the contract with myself, then I have to:

(describe a negative consequence, something you really don't like)

Or: When I do stick to my contract, I will reward myself with:

(describe a positive consequence, something that you would really like to do but don't allow yourself to at the moment)

Signed:

(name)

Hereby declares to commit to what is described in the contract. In this way, I give substance to the development of my potential and shape a life in connection to my source.

Signed thus:

(location)

On:

(date)

Signature:

NOTES

INTRODUCTION

1. Paul Ruven and Marian Batavier, *Het Geheim van Hollywood (The Secret of Hollywood)* (Amsterdam: Theatrebookshop, 2007).

CHAPTER 2

1. Irmgard Smits, *Blijf Lachen, Irmgard (Keep on Smiling, Irmgard)* (The Netherlands: West-Friesland, 1966).

CHAPTER 3

1. When peeling bulbs, the roots, skins, and glands are removed. Klisters are small bulbs located between the skirts of the large bulb. The small bulbs/klisters are the plant material for the coming season. The next autumn, the farmer will plant them on the land to grow into larger bulbs. This is how a batch of tulips, for example, is maintained. The large bulbs are used for export or sold directly to the consumer. After harvesting, flower bulbs are dried and sorted by size. The bulbs are poured onto a conveyor belt, and the sorters divide these bulbs according to size. Nowadays, this is done mechanically, but not at that time.

CHAPTER 4

1. Joe Schwarcz, "The Real Story Behind '21 Grams,'" McGill University, June 19, 2019, https://www.mcgill.ca/oss/article/did-you-know-general-science/ story-behind-21-grams.

2. Osho, *Osho Zen Tarot: The Transcendental Game of Zen* (New York: St. Martin's Press, 1994), 5.

CHAPTER 5

1. I traveled with Retreat Serendipity Travel, founded by Arthur van Laarhoven. Unfortunately, this organization doesn't exist any longer.

2. Ayahuasca Retreats Nimea Kaya Healing Center (website), accessed February 21, 2024, founded by Jill Levers. Shamans during retreat: Jorge Lopez & Rosenda Flores, Orlando Magin Matios, https://www.nimeakaya.org/.

3. "Mary and Michael Pilgrims' Way," The British Pilgrimage Trust, accessed February 21, 2024, https://britishpilgrimage.org/portfolio/ mary-and-michael-pilgrims-way/.

4. *De Kracht in Heiloo* (in Dutch), Thea Rotteveel, 2014, https://www.heiloo-online. nl/video/5079-de-kracht-in-heiloo. The documentary is about the sacred sites of Heiloo. Some believe the White Church is connected to Stonehenge. In the village, wooden circles are found. A spring is also found in the village. The water of this spring was later attributed to have medicinal properties.

5. Eric Le Gras, "*Wie Vond Het Wiel Uit?*" Trouw, June 17, 2004, https://www. trouw.nl/voorpagina/wie-vond-het-wiel-uit~b03ba520/?referrer=https://www. google.com/. Author translation: In any case, the wheels from Western Europe approach those from Mesopotamia in age, and finds from regions as far apart as the Caucasus or the land around the Indus are of a comparable age. Prof. Dr. Mamoun Fansa, director of the Landesmuseum für Natur und Mensch in Oldenburg and from Syria, undermines the idea that the wheel was invented in his native region. It rather seems that the wheel was invented in several places at the same time, including in Northwestern Europe. The time was apparently ripe for it, not only in Mesopotamia but also in other places in the ancient world.

6. Jamie Sams, *Moeder Aarde Kaarten, Spirituele Lessen uit Iindiaanse Tradities (Mother Earth Cards, Spiritual Lessons from Native Traditions)* (Haarlem, Netherlands: H.J.W. Becht, 1996).

7. Unmani: quotes during a retreat, Paris, France, August 2016, www.die-to-love.com.

8. Meetings with Jan van Delden, Sablou, France, 2017, www.janvandelden.org.

9. If you use your business car (paid with your business account) for private purposes as well, you have to pay a yearly tax for the use of your car.

CHAPTER 6

1. Wisława Szymborska: the poem "De Drie Wonderlijkste Woorden" ("The Three Most Wonderful Words"), among others included in the volume of collected poems *Einde en Begin (An End and a Start)* (Amsterdam: Meulenhof Boekerij bv, 2021).

2. Rupert Spira, retreat in San Francisco in February 2015, www.rupertspira.com.

3. *Osho Zen Tarot*, 91.

4. Bhikkhu Sanghasena, retreat in Mahabodhi International Meditation Center, July 2011, www.mahabodhi-ladakh.info.

5. Nisargadatta Maharaj, *Ik ben Zijn (I am That)* (Haarlem, Netherlands: Altamira-Becht, Haarlem, 2010).

6. *Osho Zen Tarot*, 5.

7. "Humaniversity AUM Meditation," OSHO Humaniversity, accessed February 1, 2024, https://www.humaniversity.com/social-meditations/humaniversity-aum-meditation/.

CHAPTER 7

1. Willem de Ridder, *Handboek Spiegelogie (Guide to Mirrorology)* (Netherlands: Uitgeverij de Zaak Groningen, 2004).

ABOUT THE AUTHOR

THEA ROTTEVEEL is a creative author, entrepreneur, and coach. Growing up between the tulip fields in the Netherlands and later near the harbor of IJmuiden, next to the sea, she quickly understood that what surrounds you can tell you a lot just by being quiet. For more than twenty-five years, she has been consulting for companies and institutions, helping them to understand "their why" in order to increase their impact and be successful. In addition to forging strong, diverse teams, teaching people to embrace their strengths and find their inner voice is vital in her approach to helping companies and employees flourish. In addition to being a much sought-after consultant and interim manager, she regularly makes time for creative projects. She painted, drew, and studied at the Writers' School in Amsterdam, and produced the short film *The Power in Heiloo* that was broadcast on regional TV. She is a truth speaker who likes accelerating people's paths by sharing her insights and life experiences. This is what her debut, *First-Choice Life*, is all about: an honest reflection of her inner journey. Written in a playful way, she shines her light on our growing pains.

Thea lives with her partner in Bergen (NH), an artist village in the Netherlands, and enjoys hiking through the nearby forest and dunes and along the beaches.